Angling Bumateurs

Angling Bumateurs

Book 5 in the Sell the Pig trilogy

LIVRES
LEMAS

Tottie Limejuice

Published by LEMAS LIVRES
www.tottielimejuice.com

© Copyright L.M.K. Tither 2019
Cover design DMR Creative
Cover photo © Neil Smith

ANGLING BUMATEURS

ISBN 978-2-901-77316-0

Contents

To my brother's good friend Neil

and to true, unconditional friendship

About the Author

Tottie Limejuice is the pen name of former journalist and freelance copywriter, Lesley Tither. Lesley also writes crime fiction as L M Krier and children's fiction as L M Kay.

'Angling Bumateurs' is the fifth book in the Sell the Pig series which began with 'Sell the Pig', continued with 'Is That Billinge Lump?', 'Mother Was It Worth It?', and should have concluded with
'Biff the Useless Mention'.

The first book in the Sell the Pig series is now available in French.

Tottie Limejuice is also co-author and editor of Take Three Birds, published under the collective pen-name of Jilli Lime-Holt, and the author of 'Press Releases: An Idiot's Guide - Free Publicity Through the Media'

Writing as L M Krier, Lesley has published six crime novels in the DI Ted Darling series, Baby's Got Blue Eyes, Two Little Boys, When I'm Old and Grey, Shut Up and Drive, Only the Lonely, and Wild Thing.

Under the pen-name L M Kay, Lesley's first children's novel 'The Dog with the Golden Eyes.' was published in December 2016.

Acknowledgements

Grateful thanks to my brother's friend Neil for the lovely cover shot, also to him and Jock for seeing him safely to his final resting place in such style.

Thanks, as always, to my dedicated team of beta-readers, who help to make sure my books appear with as few errors as possible. Any which remain are entirely my fault, not theirs: Jill Pennington (Alpha), Kate Pill, Alison Sabedoria, Jill Evans.

Contact Details

If you would like to get in touch, please do so at:

tottielimejuice@gmail.com

facebook.com/LMKrier

facebook.com/groups/1450797141836111/

https://twitter.com/tottielimejuice

http://tottielimejuice.com/

More from the same author

If you've enjoyed this book why not try more from author Lesley Tither under her different pen-names?

Writing travel memoirs/humour as Tottie Limejuice:

Sell the Pig
Is That Billinge Lump?
Mother Was It Worth It?
Biff the Useless Mention
Angling Bumateurs
Maman, vends le cochon

No Girl on This Train
Hobbit House in Italy

Writing crime fiction as L M Krier:

The First Time Ever
Baby's Got Blue Eyes
Two Little Boys
When I'm Old and Grey
Shut Up and Drive
Only the Lonely
Wild Thing
Walk on By
Preacher Man

Cry for the Bad Man
Every Game You Play
Where the Girls Are

Writing children's fiction as L M Kay:

The Dog with the Golden Eyes

Chapter One
17th March 2016

I knew it would come. One day. The phone call. I'd been rehearsing it in my mind, probably for a few years now. How would I react? What would I say? What would I have to do? Who would I need to inform?

Phone calls about my brother had been a feature of my life for years. Either from him, with news of the latest drama - never has the saying 'don't make a drama out of a crisis' been more appropriate than in his case - or from the police or one hospital or another, wherever he was currently being taken care of for yet another medical crisis, often alcohol-fuelled.

It had been four-and-a-half years since I'd moved out of the Pink House, where I'd lived with my mother and brother, with whom I'd moved to France in 2007. I'd finally had enough by 2011 when Mother died, aged 94, leaving me with no reason to stay. I'd tried to keep in regular contact with my brother during that time, with daily emails – sometimes up to twenty a day from him to me, fewer from me to him in return – occasional phone calls and infrequent meetings, on neutral ground. I never could face going back to the Pink House.

He'd not been doing well of late, it has to be said. His refusal, or inability, or perhaps a bit of both, to stop drinking had increased his various physical ailments and plunged him further into the dark depression from which he had long suffered. He had been making drastic efforts to cut down on alcohol but by now his system was weakened and he needed less and less to produce the same effect.

The mayor of the commune in which he lived had, for some reason, suddenly decided to take an interest in him and his welfare. He rang me up one day to say he'd been to see him and was worried about the state in which he was living. Did I know, he asked me, that it was almost impossible to get into the house, because of the piles of rubbish stacked everywhere, making access difficult?

No sh*t, Sherlock! I was tempted to say he clearly hadn't visited often, if he'd only just made that discovery. My brother's living space had always been like that, for as long as I can remember. First his bedroom in our parents' home, then his house in Wales, The Old Bakery, had been just the same. He'd also quickly converted Mother's previously neat and tidy small semi in the smart suburbs of Stockport to the same state of chaos, once she'd gone into a care home and he'd moved in.

When I lived at the Pink House, my brother confined himself to a small apartment on the ground floor, in the hopes that it would be more manageable for him. The main living area on the middle floor, where I lived with Mother, and where my brother joined us for meals and television, was always pristine and welcoming. Perhaps unsurprisingly, as soon as I moved out to live in my own little grottage (grotty cottage) the detritus had started to migrate, and had soon established itself in almost every room.

The house had become like the worst episode of Grand Designs you could possibly imagine. Perhaps Grand Designs on some sort of mind-altering chemical substance, with money no object. A lot of the problem was that my brother was not short of a bob or too. Far from it, although it was hard to believe, seeing the state of abject squalor in which he lived. And he was never short of ideas.

He was eternally planning some major project which would have needed a team of experts and a considerable amount of time to bring to fruition. Fired up by his latest enthusiasm, and on one of the upturns of his bipolar disorder, he would rush out and buy all the materials for the scheme. Or order them online, often from the UK, at vast expense because of the delivery charges. He would even start it off. There would be much squirting of spray paint to mark measurements, drilling of holes, lots of splashing of paint, literally and liberally, concrete or plaster would be mixed in over-optimistic quantities and he would go at it like a mad thing.

Then, inevitably, his mood would swing the opposite way, plunging him into the depths of depression which would see him throw teddy out of the pram along with tools and materials, and the latest brilliant idea would fall by the wayside along with its predecessors. Literally throw them out. Items costing hundreds of pounds, or Euros, depending on where he had bought them, would simply be heaved outside the door and left to rot in the rain. The plan would shortly be followed by yet another hare-brained idea, none of which were ever to see fruition.

The Pink House was large, its layout confusing. Three storeys, seven bedrooms, a bathroom and two shower rooms, a big living room, two kitchens, a laundry room and two cellar rooms, plus a large double garage. Its grounds covered nearly three-and-a-half thousand square metres. It was impressively fair-minded of my brother that he hadn't excluded much of it from his efforts.

All of this was taking a heavy toll on his physical health, not just his mental state, so hospital visits became more frequent. Those, too, followed a familiar pattern. He would meekly allow himself to be admitted for a day or two – seldom more than three – but would then be itching to get out and do his own thing once more. Once he'd dried out and been stabilised, the wild schemes suddenly seemed achievable again and he couldn't wait to get started.

Even before we'd made the move to France in 2007, I was

used to getting phone calls from the police saying they were worried about him as he had discharged himself from hospital and the medical team didn't think he was fit for release.

He was rather proud of his exploits and would recount them to me in endless rambling emails, punctuated with much ranting and swearing. On one memorable occasion, in France, he'd gone into Riom hospital as an emergency admission yet again. He was always at loggerheads with that hospital in particular, although he would eventually fall out with all of them. His system of health cover was a complicated one, dating back to his days of working for the European Commission.

In France, on admission to hospital, even as an emergency, before they will start to treat you, the hospital staff want to check that someone is going to pay them for the excellent care they are about to provide. People in Britain were recently outraged at the suggestion of producing a passport and proof of residence as soon as they set foot in hospital. Here it's routine. You're asked for your *carte vitale* (health card) and your *mutuelle* (top-up insurance) the minute you get through the door. My brother's cover required the hospital to contact his provider directly within twenty-four hours, which they usually failed to do.

He was constantly flying into a rage at their incompetence, labelling them, with his love of Spoonerisms, as Angling Bumateurs (bungling amateurs), but with one or two other, more colourful, adjectives added to the title.

Their inefficiency meant his hospital stays were a time of increased anxiety for him, not knowing whether or not the correct procedure would be followed. If not, it risked landing him personally with not inconsiderable medical bills.

On the admission in question, he told me in an email that he felt he could remain no longer, so had demanded that his outdoor clothes and shoes were returned to him. He wanted to discharge himself, rather than continue to risk staying at his own cost. The medical staff didn't want to let him go but he started threatening legal action, a favourite pastime of his. They brought his clothes but, trying to stall him, not his shoes. Undeterred, he simply climbed out of the window and ran off, barefoot, to find a taxi, fleeing back home to the chaotic familiarity of the shambles in which he lived. Or perhaps existed is a more appropriate term.

I knew he'd just had yet another admission to hospital, this time first with intestinal problems, then later transferred to a cardiac unit because his legs were swollen. He'd sent me emails to update me, and I always replied by trying to encourage him to stay in so that they could perhaps finally treat him properly.

I didn't know if his horror stories of his stay were true or just him preparing excuses to discharge himself yet again.

(sic for all) 'They have transferred me to cardiac medicine (swollen legs I suppose) it's a brighter room here but I am hungry and thirsty. A bowl of dreadful coffee at 0700, nothing all day then you might have hot drink on the evening drug round around 2200 'no we're too busy tonight dear'. The café has closed, ditto the newsagent so there is nowhere to get change for the three snack machines. M. (his friend from an English club) said he would come on Sunday so perhaps he will take the hint and bring me something if he can find a shop open. I'm connected to one of those 24hr ECG tracing machines, they say I should expect to be in here a week. Oh well!'

But inevitably, he did his usual trick of wanting a break away from the hospital, so he took himself off home. He sent me an email which was to prove poignant with its opening remark.

'I hope things are working out for you the way you want. I am just out of the hospital for the weekend, have to be back on Tuesday for colonoscopy and gastroscopy under general anaesthetic. I can't imagine them doing them both at the same time in the UK.'

I sent him a light-hearted reply to encourage him.

'Okay, good luck with that, glad you are doing something constructive at last. I think they probably do them both together now in the UK to save time and money. They probably use the same camera and if you are lucky, start with the gob end.'

I'd actually had exactly the same procedures myself as part of my diagnosis for Coeliac disease. He'd forgotten that. He was so obsessed with his own health problems that he was never very interested in anyone else's illnesses.

A couple of days after his return home, I got another email from him saying that his old cat, Felix, had died. I just hoped that this time he would manage to bury the poor thing soon, as he always had real letting go issues with his cats. I told him how sorry I was to hear the news and again encouraged him to concentrate on getting himself back to hospital and sorted out.

I didn't hear back from him, so I hoped he had taken my advice and gone back on the Tuesday as planned. Then, on the Thursday, I got a phone call.

I assumed it was going to be like so many times before, either the hospital or the police trying to track him down after he'd discharged himself. I just hoped that this time he hadn't lost all patience and escaped in his birthday suit if they refused to return his clothes, which would not have been a pretty sight. I was about to say that he would almost certainly have headed straight home and to suggest that the police contact the local *pompiers* (fire and rescue service) to go round to the house to make sure he had returned safely.

So why did the *gendarme* on the other end of the phone sound more sombre than usual as he confirmed who I was?

Then he went on, 'Madame, this is the *gendarmerie* at Combronde. I am phoning to tell you that your brother has been found dead at his house, by his cleaner.'

At the end of Biff the Useless Mention, I wrote: '...unless

something completely unforeseen happens to change my life beyond recognition, this is where the Sell the Pig series ends.'

Not entirely unforeseen, but this news was certainly set to bring some tumultuous changes to my peaceful life.

Chapter Two

The Hammer House of Horrors

Ah, that famous cleaner, who had found my brother. I had heard a lot about her from him in his emails. The sharpest knife in the drawer she apparently was not. My brother was prone to exaggeration so I wasn't sure if his tales of her ironing shirts where only the collar and placket remained intact, the rest having been chewed away to almost nothing by the many rodents inhabiting the house, were true or not.

I had been pleased to hear that, with her help, he was gradually cleaning up and that the kitchen had been transformed into something as sparkling and hygienic as an operating theatre. Or so he said. I was relieved to be able to hold on to that thought as the *gendarme* was telling me that my brother had been found dead in the kitchen. I was hoping that he had not died alone, surrounded by filth, which is what I had long feared for him.

But for now, there were practicalities to be dealt with. My brother and I together had dealt with the death of our mother. Now I was on my own to try to sort out his funeral and other matters.

The gendarme handed the phone over to *Monsieur le Maire* who told me we had met in the past. I didn't remember him. It had, after all, been nearly five years since I'd left the Pink House. I think I'd probably voted for him, when I still lived there, but I couldn't bring him to mind. I couldn't really bring very much to mind apart from the thought, turning round in my head on a loop, that my brother was dead.

First of all I wanted to know when he had died. Illogical, I know, but I didn't like the idea of him having been lying there alone for some time. The mayor said not, but he had other pressing matters on his mind. Not fish to fry, but cats to whip, ironically. That's the phrase the French use for having other things to do and there were cats a-plenty to be dealt with.

When I'd lived at the Pink House, I'd built a run in the garden to house HRH the Princess Freddie Mercury, the little half-Siamese cat who'd been born inside an old sofa on the sun terrace. She wasn't very streetwise and we'd decided not to risk her on the murderous road outside the house which had accounted for at least four of the stray cats who adopted us. When I moved away, I took HRH and her 'lady-in-waiting', Bibi, with me, leaving my brother with the two old bruisers of tomcats, Sandy and Felix.

My brother loved cats. Since my departure, he'd been gradually adding to his collection. Any waif and stray who appeared was immediately fed so, of course, realising they were on to a good thing, they would always stay.

He did his best to look after them properly, and to keep males and females separate in a growing series of outdoor enclosures he constructed. The trouble was, despite my best efforts at explaining to him how to do it, for some reason he never fully mastered the art of cat sexing. As a result, there were now at least a dozen of them and the mayor was most anxious to know what he should do with them all.

There was no question of me taking them in. I'm slightly allergic to cats, so HRH and Bibi live in the barn and are banned from the house. HRH is a strange and haughty creature. She tolerates the presence of Bibi, just, but bringing in other strange cats would, I knew, result in her hiding in a dark corner and swearing horribly for days on end. Mr Mayor was busily suggesting he should ask the APA to collect them, the animal protection society, so I gratefully agreed. It was a time for clutching at any straws on offer.

Nobody mentioned to me at the time that there would be a fee involved to take them away as it counted as an abandonment. Harsh, as my brother had clearly not chosen to die suddenly and therefore leave his cats behind. Had I been told, I would probably have told them simply to open the doors and let the cats go. They were feral, after all, and used to fending for themselves. But I thought, at the time, that I was doing the best thing for them.

The next priority was the matter of the funeral director. The mayor asked if there was one I wanted to use. I could only think of the one we had used for mother's service and cremation. I was panicking at this point, not knowing who was going to be picking up the bill as I remembered it had cost an arm and a leg.

Ever helpful, the mayor said he knew of a good and not expensive funeral director in the nearby town of Châtel-Guyon. As, clearly, my poor brother could not be left lying on his kitchen floor for much longer, I asked the mayor to go ahead and arrange for them to collect him. I would go over the following day to see them and to make all the necessary arrangements. Although I'd been expecting the news, one day, it had still been a shock and I didn't feel I had all my wits about me just yet.

Rather dreading the answer, I asked if it would be necessary for me to go over to identify my brother's body. He reassured me that he was able to do that, as indeed were the police and the fire and rescue officers who had attended, my brother having been no stranger to any of them. Also his own doctor had been summoned to certify death so there was no problem with identification.

It was a huge relief. I didn't really feel up to doing anything else taxing. My brain was still spinning from the news and I was struggling to get my head round its implications and think of all the things I now needed to do.

The most urgent issues dealt with, and the mayor holding spare keys to the property, he assured me that he would leave it secure. We arranged a mutually convenient time the following day for me to go over there.

It's always at such times that people discover who are really their good friends. I had several I knew would drop everything and come round, if I asked them to. Geographically, my French friend Domi, a former pupil in my English group, lived the nearest, but she was up to her eyes selling and clearing out her late parents' smallholding. She had a buyer and was up against an impossibly tight deadline to get it emptied.

Not only did she willingly come round to be with me, as soon as she'd peeled off her work gloves and washed her hands, she offered to drive me the following day, when I went to the house and to the undertakers.

I appreciated it even more because, as well as having the house to deal with, she works as a postie. Her work day starts at six-thirty, after a forty-minute drive to get there, and she often works six days a week. Her round is on foot, around a town with punishingly steep hills to climb and it's eleven kilometres long. Her bag of mail weighs up to twenty kilos at the start of her round and she's lucky to finish by one-thirty. She's small and slight. I wonder sometimes how she gets up the hills if they are at the start of her round when the bag is at its heaviest.

Despite all that, she arrived at my door at the appointed hour and insisted on driving me. The drive to the Pink House is about fifty miles from where I live and takes around an hour and twenty minutes, depending on traffic. I'm not usually a good passenger but I was in the state of just wanting a grown-up to take over and do everything for me. Especially one who was French and knew the French system inside out.

We were heading first for the house to meet the mayor. I

knew that what lay in store for us was not going to be pleasant. No matter how good the cleaner had been, I was doubtful that she would have been able to keep on top of things. I knew to my cost how quickly my brother could wreak havoc behind even the most thorough clean-up operations. I also knew that at least some of the cats had been living in the house and, knowing my brother, their litter trays would not have been cleaned out anything like often enough. I tried to forewarn Domi, but she was confident that, on her rounds in some of the poorest quarters of the town, she would have seen things as bad, if not worse.

I knew it would be fairly horrendous. I only realised how bad it was going to be when the mayor met us at the entrance and handed out not only blue disposable gloves worthy of a crime scene but also protective face masks.

Once we were dressed up like Scene of Crime Officers, we followed the mayor apprehensively up the stone steps to the main entrance on the middle storey. Our route took us across the patio, past the flowerbeds. All had been beautiful and well-maintained in my days there. Now it was a veritable jungle, scattered with the remnants of cat-food wrappers and other rubbish. A pile of untouched meals on wheels was stacked forlornly in a box by the front door. I knew he was getting them delivered. I didn't know he clearly hadn't been eating them, or even taking them inside, for some considerable time.

Mr Mayor used his spare keys to open up, then stepped aside to allow us to go in and take our first look at what I would quickly dub the Hammer House of Horrors.

Chapter Three
Some corner of a foreign field

We headed instinctively to the first room on the left. The kitchen. The heart of the home. My first thought was that if I ever required surgery in a French hospital, I hoped it would not be in an operating theatre prepared by my brother's 'cleaner'.

The clutter and squalor were of epic proportions, and I'd cleaned up after my brother many times before. After drunken binges, and following prolonged bouts of depression. This was something else. I stood looking, appraising it all and thinking that if we could but transport it to the Tate Modern art gallery it could make an important new exhibit, a social commentary on twenty-first century living.

For complex reasons, my brother had taken to sleeping in strange places other than bedrooms around the house. The mayor mentioned that he'd been using a mattress on the kitchen floor. The sadness of it all engulfed me. That a man so intelligent, of more than modest means, should come to this. Despite all the best efforts of all who cared for him and tried to help him. It was, and had always been, like trying to stop a train wreck by waving a red flag. It was always going to happen, one day, and now it had.

He'd recently been assigned two social workers. In his usual fashion, he'd been full of enthusiasm when he'd first met them, but the novelty had soon worn off and they'd quickly become 'the two witches'. They'd been trying hard to get him to spend some of his money to improve his living conditions, which he resisted vehemently.

'*The SS (Social services) women say I should not live like a hermit with so much money invested, the more they say that, the more I am inclined to spend nothing*', he said in an email to me. He had also become paranoid that they were conspiring to have him put under a court order which would take control of his affairs away from him.

'*Much as I appreciate their 'help' and I agree I need it, I do not want my life interfering with. I will not have a power of attorney, still less be sectioned. The only way forward is that I recover control of my own life, not hand it over to someone else. Feck off.*

He had always been paranoid about anyone touching any of his things or becoming involved in any way with how he managed – mismanaged would be more accurate – his life. All I could contribute now was to do the best I possibly could for him, preserve his privacy, and give him a send-off he would have been proud of.

Domi and I shooed the mayor out, thanking him for his efforts, and prepared to head off to the undertakers. But first I needed to find the right clothes for them to dress him in.

I knew he wanted to be cremated. I also knew, from experience with Mother, that French funerals happened quickly, within a week, so there was a lot to sort out. Practical Domi was peering into the fridge in the kitchen and saying we needed to get that emptied as soon as possible, before it started to smell.

My brother, you may remember from earlier books in the Sell the Pig series, had a major problem with throwing anything away. Anything. Ever. Even when the contents of his fridge started to move about freely of their own volition, he kept them. Perhaps for sentimental reasons. But no matter how bad the contents of this fridge were – and bear in mind some of it would have been there for at least five years, since I had left

– it would struggle to make its smell count above the incredible stench everywhere of cat pee, and worse.

One of the reasons I am more dog than cat is an illogical one. I can, and do, clean up after my dogs all the time without any problem. But cats? Different thing altogether. It takes supreme self-control to keep my stomach contents where they are meant to be when I have to do that. And a quick glance showed that it was not so much a case of litter trays not being cleaned out, more of them not being provided. Looking around, I could see that my brother had long passed the point of being able to look after himself. It was no wonder he couldn't take care of the cats as he would have wanted. Thank goodness the APA had taken them all away to a better life.

We were on the middle storey of the house, where Mother and I used to live, so I went through to the rear area, to what had been my mother's and my bedrooms and our shared bathroom. The laminated flooring in my mother's room now had a new feature – wall-to-wall fitted cat poo. I'll be kind and draw a veil over the fate of my carpeted former bedroom, and will leave your own imagination to fill in the blanks over the horrors of the bathroom.

But we had no time to linger. We needed to get to the funeral director's before they closed and I needed to find clean and presentable clothes for my brother. As well as his inability to throw anything away, he was also a compulsive shopper, an addicted impulse buyer. We often joked about his shirt-buying habit. His frequent emails to me would always say he was going shopping for food and shirts. He wasn't entirely joking. I'd already noticed there were at least six brand new unwrapped ones scattered about the kitchen floor, including four from a leading, expensive Jermyn Street tailor in Lon-don.

One of those was definitely going to be a better bet than any of the chewed though beautifully pressed ones I found hanging in the laundry room. He hadn't been exaggerating about that. The cleaner had, at least, kept his clothes in nice condition, although it was hard to see what else she had ever done for her money. I managed to find a clean, smart pair of trousers, still in the trouser press, a decent wool jacket I'd bought for him and one of his many silk ties, a navy blue and gold one I knew he'd liked to wear. I added an unopened white shirt from the heap in the kitchen.

I found plenty of new underwear, still in the packaging, as well as brand new socks, so that was all right, but it bothered me disproportionately that I couldn't find any shoes. I knew that of late his feet had become deformed, just like our mother's had, the big toes starting to turn and lie across the others. But he had always liked highly polished shoes, a throw-back to his days at sea as an officer in the Royal Fleet Auxiliary. I couldn't understand where they had all disappeared to. Unless they had all been abandoned in various hospital escapes.

I put everything I could find into a bag and we set off on the short drive to the funeral parlour, which we found easily enough. The people in charge were kind, efficient, professional. With my habit of giggling at inappropriate moments, I had to turn my eyes away from the lady with too much make-up and hope that she was not in charge of preparing the deceased for public viewing. I handed over the clothes, apologising for the lack of shoes, which I was told was of no importance.

I then asked, hoping it didn't sound too weird, if I could put a book in the coffin with him. My brother had become an unlikely fan of my crime fiction series. He'd read the first one and declared it 'bloody marvellous', which was high praise indeed, coming from him.

I knew he'd started the second one as he told me so in a phone call. The calls I had been getting from him recently had become increasingly strange, but this particular one was bizarre, even by his standards.

'I hate you,' were his opening words.

On one level, he probably did. He was certainly jealous of me. He had far more, on a material level, but I was clearly happier, though poor. It wasn't like him to express it, though. He hastened to add that he hated me because he'd just started reading my second crime fiction book and was so engrossed in it, he had no time for anything else.

I'd found it in the kitchen. He'd read a good chunk of it but not finished it. In a rare, for me, show of sentimentality, I decided to put it in the coffin with him, in some vain hope that he might find out the ending somehow.

The funeral directors were able to sort out a date while we were there and it was going to be Friday of the following week, at the crematorium in Clermont-Ferrand where we'd had Mother's. That would make it eight days, rather than a week, but cremations were on the increase in France and slots were becoming harder to get. It would be on Good Friday, which is not a Bank Holiday in France as it is in the UK, so it was business as usual at the crem.

They asked me whether his ashes were to be placed in the garden of remembrance there or transported somewhere else, which would require special dispensation from the *mairie*. In France it's not legal to keep the ashes of a loved one – or even of someone not viewed quite so fondly - perched on the mantelpiece for all eternity, as often happens in Britain.

My brother had often said whimsically that there was a corner of the garden at the Pink House where he was particularly fond of sitting. From there he could look across fields, down a valley, and there were no people or houses in sight. The trouble was, said corner was now buried under rampant brambles and rusted scrap metal. Worse, it was the likely place for a new owner to install a septic tank, which they would be obliged to do as the regulations had changed and the existing one was no longer up to standard.

To me, it seemed like possibly the most desolate place I could think of for him to spend the rest of his days, all alone. It reminded me somehow of the Rupert Brooke poem, The Soldier.

If I should die, think only this of me;
That there's some corner of a foreign field
That is forever England

My views on a possible afterlife are mixed and even I don't profess to fully understand them. My brother and I may not always have got on but I knew one thing for sure. Even I could not condemn his tormented soul to spend its days in someone else's septic tank.

Chapter Four
Best before

One of the first things I needed to do was to find the ton of paperwork necessary to accomplish anything at all in France. I would need my brother's passport, birth certificate, marriage certificate, divorce decree, death certificate and probably his inside leg measurement, just to get him cremated. The sensible French all have a special folder with such vital documents to hand. I would have to search the house to find them.

Even if I succeeded, in such a vast warren of a place, there was no guarantee the documents would be in a fit state to present to anyone official. Not after a dozen feral cats and goodness knows how many mice, rats, dormice and whatever else had used them for nests or litter trays. But I would have to try. And the first document I needed to uncover was his last will and testament.

That sounds mercenary. With my brother still in his coffin and not yet cremated, here was I wanting to get my greedy paws on his estate. It wasn't like that. It was purely a matter of practicalities.

It was going to be a nightmare to sort out his affairs. He had bank accounts in at least four countries that I knew of, though possibly with not a lot of money in some and maybe even overdrafts in others. Then there were his various stocks and shares, of which at least some were in Russia, as far as I was aware. If I was not mentioned in the will, then whoever was would be more than welcome to take over the headache and leave me out of it.

Domi had kindly volunteered to give up an afternoon at the weekend to help me make an initial foray and at least try to find some of the documents. I'd stayed in touch with two of Mother's former carers and one of them, Emilie, was on maternity leave. She also offered to come and join us and see what progress we could make between the three of us. I knew both of them were hard workers who would just get on with what needed doing without passing judgement.

The mayor met us at the house once more to let us in. I was keen to get the spare keys off him. I didn't like the idea of anyone going into the house now there was no one living there. There was no need, and I didn't want it turning into a spectator sport. I knew how much my brother would have hated that. As it was, the mayor arrived with a nosy neighbour from down the road and the famous 'cleaner', who had apparently lent my brother an electric heater which she now wanted back.

Once we'd got rid of the sightseers, Domi went to work on clearing out the fridge while Emilie started sorting through paperwork on the kitchen table. It was piled high with mail, amongst other things, much of it unopened. No doubt there were a lot of bills which would need sorting urgently. I'd decided simply to box up everything that wasn't obviously junk and take it back to my own house to be gone through later, in more agreeable and less pungent surroundings.

I also took the opportunity to do a quick recce of the whole house, to see where important documents might be hiding, and to give myself an idea of the enormity of the task ahead. The ground floor apartment, which had originally been where my brother lived, now resembled a war zone. I knew he'd had a burst water pipe at one point. He'd gone away somewhere during the cold weather and forgotten to turn the water off and drain down. There had been a burst on the top floor and everything had poured downwards, bringing down the plasterboard ceiling in his old bedroom with it.

The garage was so full of junk I couldn't get into it. I couldn't even open the doors wide enough to try and I'm not a large person. I shut them rapidly. No point in frightening myself more than I needed to.

I optimistically hoped that the top floor may not be too alarming. The intention had always been to reserve that for guests, paying or otherwise. It had three bedrooms, a shower room and loo, and I knew my brother had started to put in a kitchen of sorts, a *coin cuisine*, as the French call it, in the large, open landing space.

I was encouraged by my first sight of the upstairs living accommodation. But then, you may well remember, I am the eternal optimist. It really wasn't too bad at all. Compared to the rest of the house, it was an exhibit for Ideal Homes. One bedroom was cleared and clean, another had been turned into the laundry room and contained nothing worse than an ironing board, a steam press and a trouser press, as well as a dozen or so neatly pressed shirts, mostly full of holes.

I opened the door and went into the master bedroom, a light and airy room with a king-sized bed and stunning views from its triple window. I had an elephant in the room moment. Everything looked fine, I thought at first. Then my eyes fell on the neat but copious pile of cat poo, right in the middle of the bedspread. I couldn't face that just at the moment, so I simply withdrew and shut the door on another challenge to be faced when I felt stronger.

Several dozen bin bags full of food in various states of decay and boxes of not very fragrant documents to be sorted later, we were all three ready to head for our respective homes, pausing only to drop off the refuse sacks in communal bins on the way.

There was a lot to be done, and not a lot of time in which to do it, to organise a suitable send-off for my brother. One of the things I had to get through first was a visit to the funeral parlour to see him lying in. Not something I would have done in Britain, but quite the thing here, so I'd agreed to do it. In a sense, I needed to see him, one more time, although I knew it would be difficult.

But before I could do that, I needed to decide what the heck I was going to do with his mortal remains, as I would have to inform the funeral director as soon as possible, because of the forms needed to transport them after the cremation.

I hadn't really contacted anyone, other than the cousins in Luxembourg, to let them know of the death. My brother had few friends, but I knew he was still in regular contact with the best of them all, Neil, who lived in Kidwelly, where my brother had lived for thirty years. I still had an email address for him so, hoping it was still functioning, I sent him a brief mail to tell him what had happened.

He contacted me almost immediately and asked if we could speak on the phone. I was happy to call him and we had a nice long chat. Despite all my brother's many faults and although Neil had sometimes been the target of torrents of drunken verbal abuse and threats of violence, he'd remained his friend and was devastated to hear the news. He knew that my brother had spent about four days in hospital shortly before his death and was due to go back in again for further tests. He'd been telling Neil that he was facing the usual worries with the Angling Bumateurs who had not done the right thing with the right forms at the right time to make sure his medical fees were covered. He was concerned he was going to be facing big bills.

Neil agreed with me about not leaving him to languish in some forgotten field. I asked him whether, always supposing I could get the ashes back to the UK, he would be able to scatter him in a place which may have meant something to him. I suggested perhaps the marina at Swansea as I knew he'd liked to go there and would often take Mother there for a breath of sea air and a little picnic. I know my brother, when he was married, had always demanded to be buried at sea. But that was simply because his mother-in-law, who couldn't stand him, had always said she would dance on his grave when he died.

Neil came up with the brilliant idea of taking him on one last crazy road trip, as he and Pete had often been off on jaunts together. Between us, we decided that it should be Billinge Lump which would become his last resting place. That was the name of the landmark hill near to St Helens, the town in which my brother had been born. The Lump had such huge significance for our family, growing up, as it was always where we'd gone blackberrying as a family.

There weren't many fond memories of family life. Our father was probably in no small part to blame for the insecurities and lack of self-esteem which had plagued my brother for much of his life. It had been neither a warm nor a particularly loving family, growing up. We had been very much trophy children, to be brought out and paraded when posh friends visited, but otherwise to be criticised or ignored.

Billinge Lump had become symbolic in our family folklore. A place of happy visits as a family. The warm, rich smell of blackberries ripening on the bushes, and the knowledge that, once picked, they would quickly be transformed into delicious pies and jams in our granny's kitchen.

Neil's plan sounded like a fabulous idea. Now all I had to do was to find a way to get an urn containing my brother's ashes back from France to Neil's house in Kidwelly, all ready for its final journey.

How hard could that be?

Chapter Five
Time to Say Goodbye

One of the first things I needed to sort out was who was paying for the funeral. Although the undertaker's estimate was a pleasant surprise compared to last time, it was still more than I had in my piggy bank. Luckily, I remembered my brother telling me that the same scheme for ex-European Commission employees, as he was, which covered his healthcare would also meet the costs of his funeral.

He'd parted on bad terms from the EC when he worked for them and had finished up suing them, successfully, over the terms of his leaving. He always referred to them, amongst other things, as Angling Bumateurs and the Madhouse. He said a lot of his fragile state of mental health was due to their various incompetencies. I never knew quite how much of what he said to take with a pinch of salt, as his philosophy seemed always to be that the whole world was out of step, except him.

About ten years ago, before the move to France was even on the cards and when his lucid periods were longer, he'd sent me a detailed email about what to do if he predeceased me, and also about his assets and his plans for their disposal. I knew he'd made a will at that time, naming me, and I knew the solicitor he'd used in Wales.

The trouble was, I also knew he'd planned to change his will and had been going to see a notaire in France to do so. I didn't know if he had actually got round to doing so. The speed of his recent mood swings meant he could have done anything, up to and including leaving everything he owned to the cats' home and cutting me out altogether. That would have been fine, as long as someone other than me was going to be stuck with all the bills.

I contacted the solicitor in Wales and asked him to forward to me, as a matter of urgency, a copy of the will he had drawn up. I gave him my simplest email address, as I have a lot of different ones, which consists of four lower case letters and two numbers, so it's easy to give out. I wasn't thrilled at having to deal with this particular solicitor, especially as he was the appointed executor of the will, so everything would have to be done through him.

I'd had previous experience of him and it was not favourable. My mother had drawn up an enduring power of attorney before she lost her faculties to vascular dementia. I doubt she realised just how mentally incapable she would become and my brother and I were both relieved she had done so. It effectually gave the two of us the power to act on her behalf and in her best interest.

It caused us all sorts of stress and delays when said solicitor claimed to have no record of it anywhere, then admitted, much later, that he had been in possession of it all along but had just 'mislaid' it. He hadn't drawn it up, but it had been sent to him in connection with some other matter he was working on.

Still, considering I had sent him an email on that occasion which would probably have caused his inbox to spontaneously combust, surely he would take much greater care this time to keep track of all necessary documents.

I think that incident was in no small measure a contributory factor in my brother's paranoia about anyone from the legal profession being forcibly put in charge of his affairs. He simply had no confidence in them. It was a recurring theme in his emails to me, about not letting anyone section him or otherwise seize control of his affairs.

'I do NOT want to give my life over for someone else to manage. If ever the social services talk to you about a power of attorney or having me sectioned or anything like that, please do not agree. I might be mad but I am calm, lucid and in control. I will get there.'

Only he never did. So now it was going to be down to me to try my best to protect his interests and handle his affairs as he would have wished, to the best of my abilities.

I'll talk more about legal representatives later. They deserve at least one chapter to themselves, if not more. I'll just mention at this point that when I still hadn't received the will after nearly three weeks and called to find out why, to be told that the Welsh solicitor had taken down the email address incorrectly did not fill me with a lot of confidence. Four letters and two numbers, remember. How hard can that be?

Next a phone call to the European Commission's Social Welfare and Pension Departments to get my brother's work pension stopped and request payment of funeral expenses. They promised to send me all the necessary forms by return of post. No signs of Angling Burnateurs there so far. So now I was all set to go and say my final private goodbyes to my brother.

My kind friend Muta had offered to drive me for the occasion, rightly guessing that the return journey was not one I would like to do on my own. We'd agreed to make a bit of an afternoon of it, stopping off for coffee or afternoon tea somewhere on our way back.

First the business side of things. The undertaker and his heavily made-up assistant were kindness itself but clearly they wanted to make sure they were paid for their services at some point. I explained that the funeral costs would be reimbursed by the Commission. They told me that if my brother had a local bank and I had the RIB, they could simply deduct the cost from there and I could arrange for the reimbursement to be made directly.

French cheque books all contain several magic universal paying in slips, called a RIB in French, which have the IBAN and BIC codes of the bank account so that money can easily be transferred internationally. I did have one from his local bank but I warned them that I had no idea if there were funds available there or not.

A quick phone call by them to the bank and they were told they would be paid without fuss. All I needed to do was to ensure that the reimbursement went into the right account. Now it was time to see my brother and to report to him how things were going. If there is any kind of afterlife at all, I knew he would have been fretting about his affairs and particularly his privacy, which he had always guarded obsessively.

There was a nice suite of rooms at the funeral parlour, round the back of the building, with a pleasant sitting area and a couple of small chapels of rest, where families could spend time with their deceased loved ones. It was, of course, chilly in those. I left Muta sitting on a comfy sofa in reach of the coffee machine and went into the small, somewhat dimly lit room, where my brother was lying in his coffin.

They had done a good job of making him presentable, in his crisp, new, white shirt and silk tie. But my initial impression was of how angry he looked, despite their best efforts. I'd hoped he would have looked more peaceful, but from the set of his face, I could just see him in mid-rant, swearing at yet another demonstration of Angling Bumateurs at work. At least he was now beyond being troubled by such earthly worries. That was all down to me, from here on, unless he had appointed someone else in his will to shoulder the burden or even to take it from me completely.

I stood and talked to him for a while. I wanted to explain why I wasn't going to leave him in the corner of the garden and to tell him about the trip Neil had planned for him. I know, sentimental nonsense. Not like me. As if he could know. But it made me feel better in a way. I didn't cry. I still couldn't cry.

There was too much to be done. The time for that would come later.

When I came back out of the side chapel, Muta, that great friend, knew exactly what was needed and stood up wordlessly to give me a big hug. Then we went in search of the French equivalent of a tea shop. They're not all that common, but we were on the edge of the smart spa town of Châtel-Guyon where we were optimistic of finding the ideal thing.

Spa towns abound in this part of the Auvergne. If you're reading this in the UK, chances are that many of the bottles of mineral water on your local supermarket shelves come from around here; brand names like Vichy, Volvic, Perrier and so on are all towns in the Auvergne. Châtel-Guyon is not as well known, except to the French, but is a lovely small town. Think Buxton or Malvern, on a modest scale. Like most French spa towns, it also features a casino.

It was a pleasant and sunny spring afternoon, though not yet particularly warm. We soon found what looked like a delightful tea shop, in the main shopping street although, in typical French rural fashion, it would not be open until three o'clock. It wasn't long to wait so Muta and I spent the time walking leisurely through the small but elegant park, admiring the architecture. We also walked past the bistro where I'd seen my brother for the last time, when I'd met him for lunch with one of his new, but possibly not genuine, 'friends'. He hadn't looked too bad on that occasion. He had lost a lot of weight, but he'd told me that so it was no big shock. He was on reasonable form, too. It was a nice memory to hold on to.

Taking tea is always something of an adventure for me because of Silly Coeliac. Shops around here are not yet really geared up for people with eating restrictions. When the shop opened and we took our seats in its pleasant interior, I asked the owner if he had anything one hundred per cent gluten free. He apologised that there was nothing fresh but said he would be happy to open one of the wrapped organic cakes he had on sale, which he assured me were gluten free.

I'm paranoid about my illness. It took me a long time to get the symptoms under control so I don't take risks, at all. I asked if I might just check the ingredients on the wrapper myself, despite his assurances. It was as well I did. Not gluten free at all. Far from it. Luckily, I always carry an emergency supply of high-energy dried fruit bars which I know are safe, so I asked if he'd mind if I ate my own. He did redeem himself by producing the most delicious hot chocolate, made from scratch with real, excellent quality chocolate.

So now it was time to head home and start trying to sort everything out, including the thorny question – how was I going to get my brother's remains back to the UK after the funeral?

Chapter Six
Anything of value?

'How much??'

It was just as well I was sitting down when I received the email response to my enquiry. If I'd been standing up, I would probably have fallen over.

I'd begun my hunt for transport for my brother's ashes the logical way, searching on Google for firms who did profess-ional repatriation of remains. The first quote I'd had to fly the urn back as far as London Heathrow was more than five hundred pounds.

Like me, my brother had hated flying and avoided it as much as possible, although he had flown to places like India and Africa, as I have to the United States and Canada. I was shocked to discover that it would cost more to have his urn put into a cargo hold than it would for a live passenger to make the journey in a first class seat. And then there would still remain the problem of how to get him from London down to West Wales. That was certainly a non-starter.

Time for a Plan B.

Throw six to start again.

Not everyone likes or approves of social media. I love it! I spend a lot of time on Facebook in particular. Through it I've met a lot of lovely people, some I now call dear friends. There are, of course, those who, on the strength of a few exchanges online and perhaps reading one or two of my books, feel they know me better than I do myself and therefore feel entitled to tell me how I should live my life. But in the main, I do enjoy the interaction. It's also an incredible place for finding help for strange things, often from the most unexpected quarter.

Time to throw out there, into social media world, the most bizarre request I'd had to make to date. Is anyone going back to the UK soon who might have room in the boot of their car for the ashes of my late brother? Guaranteed to behave himself, apart from a fondness for *risqué* jokes, though with a long history of being travel sick.

It was touching, and surprising, that I got quite a few offers, some from complete strangers. One came from a lovely lady called Laura, with whom I had chatted, on and off, on Facebook, for some time previously. We seemed to be in tune on many things, particularly environmental issues. She was heading for Brighton, on dates which fitted perfectly, and would be delighted to take my brother with her, as long as she could convince her husband of the legality of it.

I had to chuckle, imagining the conversation.

'Oh, by the way, *cheri*, when we pack the car, we'll be including the ashes of the brother of someone I've never met. But don't worry, it's all perfectly legal and not a cover for drug-running.'

It looked as if it would all work out. I just had to find a way of getting him up to her house, as she lived four hours' drive in the wrong direction. Google assured me that it was perfectly legal to send someone's ashes through the post, as long as they were accompanied by the correct paperwork. So off I trotted to the post office to find out the cost.

I decided not to go to the one in my local small town of Olliergues. At some point, I was going to have to declare what would be in the mysterious parcel I wanted to send. I just didn't want it gossiping about in my home town that the strange, mad, English hippy woman from up the hill was posting body parts. Instead I went to the larger one in my normal shopping town, Courpière.

Post offices here are very different to those in Britain. For a start, there are no glass screens at the counters, except, perhaps, in much bigger towns. It came as something of a shock when security measures were put in place at the little Olliergues post office, after a robbery at a nearby rural one. It's so small that there is only one person working at a time. Our regular person is a small lady with very short hair, coloured the dark auburn shade beloved of so many French women of a certain age. She is so stern it would have to be a brave armed robber to venture in before her strict gaze. But just in case, customers now have to press a buzzer at the door and, as long as you have her approval, which is not guaranteed, she unlocks the door.

You also have to press something like a light switch at the side of the door, perilously close to the fire alarm button, to let yourself out. Of course, none of us are used to this performance yet so we all regularly walk head first into the locked glass door, nearly concussing ourselves in the process.

Once inside, there is no standing docilely in a line behind a rope, waiting for a disembodied voice to say, 'Cashier number six, please.'

I've never known any people as good and as polite at queuing as the Auvergnats. Nobody jumps queues, unless they're foreign, or an outsider, and everyone keeps track of whose turn it is. People even notice if someone is clearly in more of a hurry than they are and happily make way for them.

The Courpière post office would be a bit more anonymous for my strange enquiries, at least. There were usually three people working in there, two men and a woman, although it's barely the size of my kitchen. The big disadvantage is that, being so small, and all open, there is absolutely no privacy. So unless it was empty when I went in, I was going to get some strange looks from other customers, as well as the staff.

I'd found out from the funeral director the dimensions of the urn and also its approximate weight once filled. Clearly it needed to go by recorded delivery, to make sure it arrived safely at its destination and wasn't lost in some sorting office somewhere. The helpful man behind the open counter asked me about insurance. Would there be anything of value in the parcel?

The look on his face was priceless when I told him the package would contain my brother's ashes. He took some convincing that it was legal to do that. It was clearly the first time in his career with La Poste that he'd encountered such a request. But he remained perfectly polite as we discussed the most secure method of sending the parcel, and the costs involved.

So that was my brother's transport arranged as far as Brighton. Next, I had to get him onward-bound from there across the country to Wales. His friend Neil was not going to be able to take him on the road trip for a few weeks, possibly months, yet. He had a serious back injury and was waiting to hear whether or not it was going to require surgery.

Back on to Facebook to see if, by any chance, anyone could provide a lift from Brighton to Kidwelly for my brother. This time the offer came from an old friend, one you may remember from previous books. One, in fact, to whom Book 4 of the Sell the Pig trilogy is dedicated. Robin. Stupid Boy! Also known as Pig Boy, because at the riding school where we both worked in our teens, the favourite pastime of myself and the other staff, mostly girls, was to throw said Pig Boy into the pig pen to see if he could actually run faster than a grumpy Gloucester Old Spot boar.

People often ask me why he and I appear to dislike each other so much and if so, why do we stay in contact. It's a British thing. Generally, the more we like someone, the more we heap insults on their head. Robin and I are actually fond of one another, though I doubt either of us would admit to it in public on social media. I taught him to ride when he was an annoying small boy. He's now an annoying large boy, but we are still good friends.

He lives in London but could, he said, easily have a run out to Brighton to meet Laura and collect my brother. He could then keep him safely at his house until Neil was ready to receive him, then post him on his way. So everything was in place for his final journey.

It was to be Robin who once again came to the rescue to help me with music for the funeral, the organisation of which was next on my expanding 'To Do' list. I knew exactly what songs I wanted played for the funeral but technically-minded I am not. I can do basic stuff with a computer. I've worked via the internet for years. But it really is basic.

I had no idea how to go about finding and downloading the music from a non-pirating site. As I regularly lose royalties for my books because of sites which illegally offer free downloads of .PDFs of my work, I refuse absolutely to go down the route of robbing other artists of theirs. So any source I used would have to be legitimate. My brother had been in charge of that side of things for our mother's funeral. Luckily Robin rose to the occasion and helped me out with what I needed. I thanked him by going a whole day without calling him Stupid Boy, in public, at least.

So the next challenges to be faced were the funeral and then collecting the ashes afterwards. After that, it would be on to the serious business of trying to sort out his financial affairs, with no doubt endless unpaid bills to be dealt with. Not to mention the worrying question of where was I going to find a buyer for a large house covered in cat poo and stinking to high heaven? Not to mention a small, elderly electric car which only ran when it felt like it, and a big and battered old motorhome which had definitely seen better days.

Chapter Seven
He ain't heavy

My brother's powers of logical thought had been rapidly deserting him of late. He'd always been highly intelligent and well able to apply the principles of Occam's Razor – all things being equal the simplest explanation requiring the fewest assumptions is usually the correct one. All that had gone by the wayside recently. It had become impossible to have much of a rational dialogue with him at times.

I'd regretfully had to tell him to stop phoning me. I had enough problems of my own to deal with. He had two social workers helping him, and I found his calls too draining, because they just kept going round in circles.

What led up to my request was the time he called me about his new wood-burning stove. He said it was burning too fiercely and he was afraid of a chimney fire. He was thinking of calling out the *pompiers* to put it out for him. He'd done volunteer fire service training himself when he worked in Brussels, so I patiently reminded him of the fire triangle – Oxygen/Heat/Fuel. Take away any one of the three and the fire would go out without the need for intervention.

I knew he had a habit of over-stoking fires. He always tended to put far too much fuel on at once, even leaving the door open as it wouldn't close because of the quantity of firewood. No wonder his wood-burner was roaring away! I patiently explained that my fancy new kitchen range, Leo the

Lohberger, was exactly the same. I had to feed Leo one good-sized log at a time then wait for that to burn almost to nothing before adding another, otherwise I practically had to sit in the garden because the heat output was so intense.

When he started wailing about wanting to be able to put as much wood on at a time as he chose, I had to end the conversation because it was doing my head in. It was, sadly, the last time we actually spoke in person, although we continued to exchange emails up until shortly before he died.

I didn't often buy him presents, it has to be said. That's not as mean as it sounds. He just had far more money than I, so he could, and did, buy himself anything he wanted. Nor was he a gracious recipient of gifts. When I did get him something, often going to great lengths to track down a particular item, it would usually get tossed aside, often unopened, never to be mentioned again.

Perhaps it was my strange, prophetic powers at work, but I did get him something nice for what was to be his last Christmas. He'd asked me about a song he'd heard on our local radio station, *France Bleu Pays d'Auvergne*. It was a beautiful and haunting piece called Corsica, sung by Patrick Fiori and Patrick Bruel. I'd heard it and loved it. I bought him the CD and sent it to him with a little card signed, in my usual fashion, with a single 'x' for a kiss after my name.

Innocuous enough. But in his befuddled state, my brother told his 'friend', the one he'd met at the English language club, that I'd never signed anything with an 'x' before so that clearly signified that I was about to do away with myself. He didn't actually contact me to see if that was the case. I got all this third-hand through said friend who had, to be fair, been trying to keep an eye on my brother, to the best of his ability. I did, however, on the one occasion I had met him, think he seemed rather more interested in the legendary millions my brother often boasted of, which were nothing more than a Walter Mitty fantasy.

I found the CD amongst a heap of junk in the kitchen at the Hammer House of Horrors, unopened, never played, once I started clearing up. I certainly wanted that particular track played at his funeral, as I knew he liked it. In his usual fashion, when I mentioned that particular story on Facebook, Robin couldn't stop himself from his little joke; 'Ve haf vays of making you listen to your Christmas present'. I think some people who don't know us well nor understand our shared sense of humour were a bit upset by that.

I guessed there wouldn't be many people at the funeral, but I wanted it to be meaningful, and those who came, certainly the English ones, would want to sing something. My brother had enjoyed singing. He'd had lessons for a time. I knew one of the tenors he admired was Josh Groban, so I picked his version of 'You Raise me Up' as a piece we could all sing, then added Andrea Bocelli's *Con te partirò*, known in English as 'Time to Say Goodbye', for the end of the service.

Although there weren't likely to be many people attending, I was determined to make it as good a send-off as I could. Muta had kindly agreed to drive me to the crematorium. She, like me, is pathologically punctual, so I knew she wouldn't be on the last minute, letting me get into a flap in case we weren't there on time.

As it was, we arrived early, so we sat together in the vestibule drinking good but inexpensive hot chocolate from the nearby vending machine, greeting people as they arrived.

My brother's friend from the English club was there, as were my English friends, Geoff and Christine. Two of the ladies from the language group I used to run at the Pink House, with whom I had kept in touch, kindly came, as well as the mother of the two girls from the group, now grown up and away at university.

The mayor didn't come, despite his protestations of being a good friend of my brother, nor did anyone else from the village. It was Good Friday so it was just possible that people were busy doing family things for the Easter weekend. It was still bad form that neither the mayor nor any of the deputies attended.

The little service went well. I'd carefully prepared a short address, in French, as all those present spoke French. It was brief but, I hope, to the point. I said my brother had been a *bon viveur*, who enjoyed telling a good tale but who had probably never been truly happy, which I think summed his life up quite well. He was only sixty-seven when he died.

His great friend Neil had not been able to get over for the funeral but he and his other half had their own mini ceremony for him back in Kidwelly, playing the same pieces of music at the same time as the funeral was taking place, connecting through the ether.

Once the formalities were over, Muta, Geoff, Christine and I did exactly what my brother would have wanted us to do – we went out for a good lunch. Domi had kindly agreed to go to my house to let the dogs out for a pee break, as I had no idea how long I would be. Fleur is good with anyone and everyone and even nervous Rosie had decided that her *tata* Domi was a friend who could be trusted, so I was not too anxious about them.

I still hadn't grieved. Not properly, though there had been a fair bit of sniffing at the music choices for the ceremony, and not just from me. At the moment, I was still too numb. It would come.

Life was going on as normal all around me. Three days after the funeral, the first cuckoo arrived back from his winter holidays in Africa, shouting his presence to the world. Of all the returning migratory birds, the cuckoos are my least favourite, and not just because of their incessant, unchanging call. They're a horrible parasitic bird, with the birth of each one being responsible for the death of at least one other of a different species. But still we tend to measure the arrival of spring by their infernal cuckoo-cuckoo-cuckoo.

The next milestone to be passed was going to collect the ashes. I opted to do that on my own, although friends offered to come with me. I knew it was going to be hard and I'm a strangely private person, for someone who bares all in memoirs. It was something I preferred to do by myself. Just me and my brother together, one last time.

You may remember, from previous instalments, my brother's belief that we, as a family, are cursed. I was starting to wonder if he had something when I drove to the funeral parlour to collect his ashes and found the road closed for cable-laying. It wouldn't normally matter but it was pouring with rain, not pleasant to have to leave the van and sprint, never one of my strong points, the short distance, almost falling into a yawning, water-filled ditch as I did so.

I'd gone armed with all the mountain of paperwork required for collecting ashes, including details of the make, model and registration number of Laura's car in which my brother would be travelling, because that would be in a different *département*. Movement of ashes is strictly controlled, other than in the post.

When they finally handed me the urn, I was shocked. I'd handled the one containing my mother's remains. This felt lighter, if anything, and she had been tiny. It brought home to me just how much weight he had lost and how insubstantial a thing his life had become. And it inevitably gave me one of my famous earworms, the one from The Hollies: 'He ain't heavy, he's my brother.'

On the way back, I drove to a picnic spot which he often used to visit, to admire the stunning view. It was somewhere I'd often stopped for a cup of tea on my way back to the Pink House at the end of my R&Rs days. I'd even wild camped there in my van on more than one occasion.

I put the urn on the dashboard, where he could admire the scenery one more time, then brewed myself a cup of tea from my trusty flask. He must have done the same thing in the same place so many times. Then I cried. I cried until I had no more tears left. When I'd done I drove him back to my house, for his first ever visit, before taking him to the post office the next day.

Chapter Eight
The Three Soliciteers

Nothing involving my brother was ever simple. That was unlikely to have changed simply because he had shuffled off this mortal coil. As the song says, 'There may be trouble ahead...'

I'd now received a copy of the will he'd made some ten years previously, when he was still in Wales, and a phone call to his local solicitors in France had revealed that he hadn't made one since. That meant that, apart from some small bequests to his friends, I was the sole beneficiary. That sounded fine in principle. The practice was to turn out to be something of a poisoned chalice, and a highly costly and complicated one, at that.

His 'friend' from the English club was still sniffing round, sending me emails. On a hunch, I told him that there were no hidden millions (true), probably not much money (true) and a stack of unpaid debts (sadly also true). Funnily enough, his interest seemed to wane at that point and, apart from one email inviting me to keep in touch if I wanted to, but bizarrely addressed to someone called Karen, whoever she might be, that was the last I heard from him.

The saga would see me having to engage not just one, not two, but three solicitors. To be precise, two solicitors and a *notaire*. One in Wales, one in England and one in France. Hence the Three Soliciteers. Athos, Porthos and Aramis they were not. I doubt they could buckle a swash between the trio of them. More like Chico, Harpo and Groucho, the Marx Brothers.

In the interests of avoiding a claim for defamation, I don't intend to say anything which might identify them. They will simply be referred to as Mr Wales, Mr England and Me France. In France, all lawyers take the title *Maitre*, abbreviated to Me.

My brother was not rich, by any stretch of the imagination, but he did have assets. Not least of which was the famous 'big six-wheeler, scarlet-painted, London Transport, diesel engine, ninety-seven horsepower omnibus.

'Hold very tight please, ting ting.'

In case you're not familiar with the lyrics, or think I have lost the plot slightly more than usual, it's an old Flanders and Swann song about a London bus. And my brother had precisely that; a 1960s Leyland Routemaster, which had done its service on the Oxford Street route in London's West End. That, along with bits and bobs of accounts in several different countries, meant that it was not going to be the easiest of estates to administer.

Before his faculties had deserted him too much, my brother had made an attempt to get his affairs in order and had sent me an email detailing his intentions. In it, he told me he had appointed Mr Wales as enduring attorney over his affairs and added, *'Some feel it is a great honour to bestow to appoint a relative as an attorney. It's not. It's a pain in the fundament and f*cking hard work.'*

He'd also sent me a form of who to contact about his pension and funeral expenses on his demise, noting in the covering letter, *'No doubt it is just a coincidence that this "what to do when someone dies" letter from the Madhouse came in the same post as my blood group card from the hospital!'*

I'm an optimist by nature, always trying to look on the bright side. But I have to confess I was struggling to find a bright side knowing that everything would have to be handled by a solicitor who had not been able to take down correctly an email address comprising four letters and two numbers.

Mr Wales was in a small town in a largely rural area. I wasn't unreasonable enough to expect him to be fluent in French and to have an intimate knowledge of France's complicated Napoleonic laws. He would, after all, be bi-lingual English/Welsh, living and practising where he did. The trouble was, it became clear from the outset that he was not very bright and unable to cope with anything outside his immediate field of expertise. Which was actually more of a small vegetable plot than a field. A back garden, perhaps. Or maybe a window box.

To be fair, it wouldn't be every day he would have had to administer an estate which included a double-decker bus. But his lack of basic knowledge was a worry, from the beginning. When I said I had no idea of the whereabouts of the bus's documents, log book and so on, he claimed it would therefore be impossible to sell it. In the end, it was quicker and simpler for me in France to download from the internet and send to him the request form for the Driver and Vehicle Licensing Authority in Swansea to issue a duplicate. A perfectly simple, relatively inexpensive and routine action. In fact, his office is probably less than ten miles from the DVLA's offices. And this was someone who would be charging me two hundred pounds an hour for his time.

He also considerably annoyed me by beginning his initial emails to me with 'Hi' like some Cliff Richard fan, then addressing me by my first name. I've been in France long enough to squirm at such familiarity. French is still very formal. A common sign-off for a letter is, 'Please accept, Sir, Madam, the expression of my distinguished salutations.' Official letters, such as from a *notaire* to their client, most definitely do not begin with the equivalent of 'Hi'.

It also didn't help that he used the wrong spelling of my name, and that of Mr England, until I pulled him up sharply on both accounts.

Because my brother had assets in different countries, and a British will, I had no idea which country would take precedence over it all. But I knew a man who would.

Mr England came from a firm of bi-lingual solicitors, qualified in French and English law, who specialised in helping Britons abroad with just such matters. I was clearly going to need to engage his services and tap into his expert knowledge on the subject.

Another two hundred and fifty pounds an hour.

Kerching!

He was, unlike Mr Wales, professional and efficient, but he had bad news for me. Because my brother was resident in France, all his affairs would come under French administration, and that would mean we needed to engage the services of a French *notaire*. I didn't even want to know what that was going to cost. Some things were best left in the dark.

There was even more bad news. Had the will come under UK law, there would have been no inheritance tax to pay, as the amount was well below the threshold. But France is a country of notoriously high taxation, hence its good services and infrastructure.

Furthermore, the usual line of succession here is generally considered to be parents to children. In fact parents aren't allowed to disinherit their offspring. Taxation from one spouse to another or to children is moderate. Anyone outside that line, including siblings, and it becomes punitive. I was told I would be facing tax of between forty-five and sixty per cent of the assets. Even more alarmingly, it was payable before I got my hands on anything which might be left over after the vulture-lawyers had taken their fill.

My poor brother! He had no idea of the nightmare he was leaving me. He'd not done his homework on the tax issue and had always assumed I would be well provided for. Or perhaps he'd simply thought that, his income from the EC being tax-free because he had diplomatic immunity, his estate would not be taxed, either. I did have the choice of refusing to accept the inheritance and simply walking away, leaving the state to deal with it all.

The problem was, my brother would have hated the idea of strangers in his house, going through his things. He was, by now, safely sitting on a shelf at Robin's place in London, doing a good job of covering up a stain on the wallpaper, by all accounts. Depending on your beliefs, there would have been no reason to suppose he would know what was going on with his things since his departure.

But I would know. Just from my initial rummagings, I had found out things about him and his sad life I had not known before. They were not things to be shared with anyone, except of necessity with loyal friends, who had volunteered to help me.

I might not have been able to do enough for him during his lifetime, but I could certainly do this for him now. No one but me and my most trusted friends would ever know all of his secrets. No state official would set foot over the threshold of his home. And before ever I put it on the market, I would do my level best to present it in a neutral way, with all his personal possessions and signs of squalor carefully removed so nobody could judge him.

Footnote: As I'm editing this chapter, I have just heard that d'Artagnan needs to join the team. That's right. I need a fourth soliciteer. This is because one of my brother's bank accounts was located in Jersey, in the Channel Islands, and since he didn't live on the island, it requires a separate grant of probate there to recover that money.

Another twelve hundred or so pounds.

Another kerching.

This came to light in an email from Mr Wales who wrote to tell me, in tones of wonderment, that it was necessary because my brother was domiciled in France, as if this were some new and amazing revelation.

Keep in mind that, when I got this email, ten months had elapsed since my brother's death. The French authorities had already ruled that he was domiciled in France, which was why I had already paid out a truly eye-watering sum in taxes, having had to cash in all my meagre savings and empty all my piggy banks to do so.

So, no sh*t Sherlock? He was domiciled in France? I didn't know that.

I am starting to wonder if my dogs, Fleur and Rosie, couldn't have done a better job than Mr Wales, and neither of them speaks much English.

Chapter Nine
It's a long, long road

So says The Hollies' song. And before purists jump on me, that's from the last verse. The opening line is, 'The road is long.' Whichever, it was very apt for the amount of miles which lay ahead of me over the coming weeks and months. And it was an appropriate song as The Hollies once had a boutique in Stockport, where my brother and I grew up.

The Pink House, or, as I had rechristened it, the Hammer House of Horrors, after the horror films from the famous studios, was about fifty miles from my grottage. With good binoculars, I could just about pick it out from up by the church I call St Loo and St Dongle, just up the road from my house. Depending on traffic, it took me between one-and-a-quarter and one-and-a-half hours to drive there by the back roads, much more pleasant and less costly that the motorway route as there are tolls on lots of the motorways here. But then, we don't pay an annual road fund licence, as in Britain, so it balances out in terms of cost.

I was going to have to do many trips there to make it even remotely presentable in order to have it valued. I knew it was probably going to be worth less than half of what my brother had paid for it without considerable work and industrial cleaning. I simply didn't have the means to pay professionals, and there was only so much I could do, either alone or with the help of friends, to make much difference.

The most urgent thing was to get over there and get rid of the worst of the cat poo, followed by sloshing round a gallon or two of disinfectant and opening all the windows. Oh joy! Cleaning up after cats. My least favourite job of all.

Thank goodness my Mother Nature always rises to the occasion and helps me get through the difficult times. Each time I made the drive, which seemed to get longer on every occasion, she would find something wonderful to show me to lift my flagging spirits. A hunting Montagu's harrier, a cheeky red squirrel skipping across the road, a pair of shy roe deer, even a circling osprey on a couple of occasions. It certainly helped.

I soon reached the point where, although it was still horrendous, it was at least possible to go in the house without breathing apparatus. I could now, finally, get a couple of estate agents to come and take a look. I wanted them to give me an approximate idea, not only of a sale price but of the likelihood of finding a buyer at all, at a time when the housing market was as flat as the proverbial pancake. Especially as the market to Brits had effectively collapsed, along with the pound.

On the plus side, it was a huge house with a big garden, boasting wonderful views. It was structurally sound, although needing a fair bit of cosmetic work to bring it up to habitable standard. The area was relatively sought-after, with good roads and a motorway not five minutes away.

The definite minus was that any viewers needed a strong stomach and plenty of vision to see beyond the current sorry state it was in, despite my best efforts so far.

I thought the most sensible course of action would be to get a valuation as it stood, in all its cat-pee-impregnated glory, as that would give me a worst case baseline figure to work from. But before I could do that I needed to make sure any estate agent could actually physically get into most parts of the house and would not be rendered unconscious by the smell.

My brother had been a great one for dabbling in stocks and

shares. I'd never dared, as it's way outside my knowledge and comfort zone. If I had been looking for an investment, I would have put money into the bin bag production market. I must have kept it afloat single-handedly for a few months, with the quantities I was having to buy.

I hate throwing things away for them to end up in landfill and try hard to recycle everything possible. My brother just hated to throw things away, full stop. Some of the piles of old newspapers I found pre-dated his move to France, so he had brought them with him from Wales. He always claimed he kept them as he might want to read them one day. Of course, he never did.

With his obsessive shopping habits, especially when on a high with his bi-polar disorder, the local charity collecting bins for clothing were going to do well out of him. I practically filled a large one of those on every trip I made, with good quality shirts, more silk ties, jackets, dinner jackets, suits and all manner of things.

My poor little Kangoo van needed new rear shock absorbers with the amount of stuff I was stuffing in the back on each visit, which cost me a couple of hundred euros. Anything that could be recycled was. Unfortunately there was far more stuff which just had to be thrown away than I would have liked. Hence all the bin bags I had to buy. But each bag filled represented a bit more of the house cleared, another square foot of floor revealed, so more of a prospect of a sale.

Some days I would go for the full day and do a run to the recycling bins and tip near to the house. Fleur and Rosie went to the lovely nearby kennels for those days, so they were not left alone. They liked it there and got on well with the lady in charge. I liked it as she always posted photos and videos of the dogs being exercised in the two-hectare park with its high deer fencing, so I knew they were secure and having fun.

I would take a picnic with me and always go somewhere other than the house to eat it. There was a particular place from where I could look across to the spot in which my grottage nestled in the foothills of the Forez mountains. It was comforting for me to look at it and know I would soon be back in its sanctuary, with my dogs.

I developed the habit of talking to my brother as I worked. It made me feel better, somehow. It started on the drive over, as my route took me through Crevant-Laveine, the village where we had so nearly bought the house with the hamman, before settling on the Pink House instead.

'Oop north', where my brother and I came from, a way of referring to a sibling is 'our kid', sometimes regionally pronounced more like 'are kid'.

'Crev-Lav, are kid, remember?' I'd begin, as I drove through it.

Then, shortly after there, once the big white building which housed a sausage factory, just down the road from the Hammer House of Horrors, came into my sight, I would tell him I wasn't far away and would be there soon. Then I'd tell him of my planned projects for the day; what I hoped to achieve. I tried to keep my plans realistic, achievable, so I could always finish the day feeling positive, having reached my goals.

Once inside the house, I'd chat away to him, to keep my spirits up. I tried to make a joke of it all, especially his collecting habit. Otherwise I would have found myself submerged by the sadness of it and unable to carry on, especially alone.

'Wow, amazing, are kid. A spirit level! I'm so glad I found that. I've only found eleven of them so far, and you can never have enough spirit levels, I always say.'

The thing I found perhaps the saddest of all was the many self-motivation signs he had printed, laminated and put up around the place.

'Stop drinking', said one. As if it were that simple. Although I was surprised by how little alcohol and how few empties I found in the house. He had clearly been making an effort.

The one which affected me the most deeply was something he had clearly copied from some social media site and printed out. I'd never thought of us as all that close – not until I read this:

'Your sister is your first female friend in life. No-one will ever understand your craziness like your sister. Even if you don't get together or talk as much as you'd like, she always remains your friend. While people come and go in your life, your sister will always be in your heart for a lifetime. It's National Sisters week, so share if you have a sister that you love with all your heart.'

Eventually, I reckoned I had shifted enough bin bags and sprinkled enough disinfectant so that I could get the estate agents round. The first was young and keen, dressed more for a garden party than for tiptoeing around the Hammer House of Horrors. Even with all the windows and doors, on all three floors, wide open, it was still decidedly whiffy, but considerably better than it had been.

She was enthusiastic but I felt her estimation was optimistic and I needed realistic. I wanted rid of the house as soon as I possibly could, even if that meant taking a hit on the price.

The second agent was older, wiser and probably much nearer the mark, with her lower estimate. She'd been recommended to me by a French friend. She'd been in business locally a long time and was still going. She was the more likely of the two to know the current market.

I wasn't planning to put the house on the market yet, at either price. I just needed a figure for Me France to calculate the amount of the estate and therefore to work out how many arms and legs the French taxman was going to be demanding from me in payment. I was also a long way from being in a position to sell it yet, as it would be some time before probate was granted in Britain and the equivalent went through in France.

I also needed to be absolutely sure that the estate I had inherited would at least be solvent before I accepted it. The last thing in the world I wanted to do was to put myself in a position where I could potentially lose my own home by running up huge tax bills and not having the means to pay them, other than by selling up.

And all of that meant having to do some serious sums. My worst subject. Frankly, Rosie could do a better job with arithmetic than I could.

Chapter Ten

Weshiftanyshite.com

With all that I had going on at the moment, there was not going to be much time to go off on any of my usual little jaunts. By coincidence, my good friend Alex was equally as busy, though with nicer things, such as his seventieth birthday. He simply didn't have enough free time in one chunk to make his usual month-long annual pilgrimage, so it would have to go on hold until next year.

I had very few family members left in the UK, just a handful of cousins I hadn't spoken to for years. I managed to find their contact details to let them know about my brother. We did the usual post-bereavement thing of promising to stay in touch, all of us knowing it would probably never happen. I wasn't sure if Mother's remaining sister, my aunt, was still alive. She would be well into her nineties if she was so could probably survive her remaining years without knowing the news about my brother, if she even remembered who he was. The last time I had phoned her, she'd been a bit confused over names and who was related to whom.

I'd always kept in contact with some of my cousins in Luxembourg, if only with the annual Christmas card and Round Robin newsletter of what was going on in my world, and reading of their latest news. I hadn't seen them in ages, and they had never visited me here in France. By one of life's bizarre coincidences, two of them had decided to spend a holiday in May in the Cantal region of the Auvergne. At the designated Most Beautiful Village of Salers, to be precise, where Alex and I had enjoyed a short break the year before. They promised to call on me on their way back.

It was one of my twin cousins, Mady, who would be visiting with her husband, Ernest. Her father had been my father's cousin, which I think makes us second cousins, although I'm never sure about such things. Ernie had run the farm where my grandmother had been born, after her father retired and before he took his own retirement. They could only manage a flying visit but kindly offered to take me out to lunch when they came. I needed no second bidding. All treats were most welcome.

I'm lucky in that one of the best restaurants I've eaten in anywhere is less than ten minutes from my house, in the village of Augerolles. Lovely people, amazing local produce, beautifully cooked, and no worries at all for me eating there and managing my Silly Coeliac. They knew me well by now and would vet every item on the menu to tell me what I could and couldn't eat. It made a pleasant change from being met with blank looks and me having to explain and check.

Spring so far had been a disappointment, uncharacteristically and unrelentingly wet and miserable. It was to prove good news for the grape crop, after a hot summer to follow, but less so for most fruit and vegetables which had a poor year, with the consequent hike in prices.

I always hoped for fine weather when visitors came. My little grottage is compact and *bijou* but also on the dark side, as are many houses here, built with the intention of keeping out hot sunshine through the summer. I always preferred to be able to entertain sitting outside on the deck, with the glorious views of the volcanoes. But it was definitely not outdoor weather, so we were stuck indoors for our pre-lunch *apéros*.

It was a flying visit, with a long drive north ahead of them, but it was nice to catch up with relatives and to share memories of my brother. He'd been to stay with them a couple of times since the move to France but I hadn't seen them in twenty years or more, since I'd taken my mother to visit them one time.

We had a wonderful lunch, as usual, and they were suitably impressed by the quality of the food and the value for money. I've almost started to take it for granted, though not quite. I know how much Alex has struggled to find anything which comes close, on his return from holidays here, and he lives in Britain's second city, Birmingham.

To stop myself turning into a total hermit, I generally managed to catch up weekly with at least one of my friends living in the area, usually Muta. It's always nice to have a good natter and forget all that's going on. Domi's visits helped enormously, too, when her English lessons took the form of working through my crime fiction series as set books, with ensuing hilarity at the slang expressions. And then there was another visit to look forward to.

Best friend Jill, supportive as ever, had kindly offered to bring her annual visit dates forward from the usual time and to stay a few days longer than she usually did, to give me a hand with anything that needed doing. It wouldn't exactly be our usual fun and games week of outings, picnics and meals. But it would be a huge physical and emotional boost for me to have some company. I knew Jill wouldn't turn a hair at the smell of cats, as her parents had kept seventeen of them at once, at one time.

She was most insistent that I should make the best possible use of her while she was with me, with as many trips to the Hammer House of Horrors as needed to achieve some visible degree of progress. It was a kind offer, but I was also determined to use her visit as an excuse to have some fun, which had been lacking of late.

I was making progress at the house, although probably only I would have noticed it. I always set myself realistic targets on every trip I made, never more than I knew I could achieve in the time I'd allowed myself. Being overly optimistic and trying to do too much had been my brother's weakness. If he had taught me anything, it was to keep it manageable and finish each visit with a sense of achievement, rather than failure.

There was so much which needed doing that it would have been easy to get distracted and not see any signs of improvement, so I stuck to my game plans. I'd discuss them with my brother as I worked, and as soon as I felt my attention wandering, I'd bring myself up short with a firm, 'One job at a time, Tottie, you silly tart. One job at a time.'

I went to collect Jill from the airport at Clermont-Ferrand, as usual. An early evening arrival which was considerably delayed, without those of us waiting knowing the reason. But eventually Jill was walking through the arrival gates, pulling her faithful wheeled luggage behind her, smiling, as ever, and looking her customary imperturbable self which had earned her the nickname of Sensible Aunt Jill, although she is four days younger than me, and never lets me forget it.

We awarded ourselves a quiet first day of dog walks and relaxing, gearing up for the horrors to come, when we certainly planned to be shifting a lot of shite.

There is a particularly annoying British television advert for buying used cars, with a silly one-note jingle of Webuyanycar.com. On Jill's first visit, when she was confronted with the full scale of what she had volunteered her services for, we both got a fit of the giggles, encouraging one another with chants of Weshiftanyshite.com. It amused us both so much that I had T-shirts printed for us with the slogan on.

Our first trip to the Hammer House of Horrors was to be a full day, so the dogs were going off to the doggy kindergarten, to have fun. I'd arranged to hire a van from the local Intermarché supermarket. A Ford transit, so it was bigger than my little Kangoo, and we planned to concentrate on shifting only stuff which was too large, bulky or cumbersome for me to attempt to move by myself. Things like a cement mixer which looked as if it had only been used once before the novelty wore off, which I could hopefully sell on to recuperate at least the cost of hiring the van.

We certainly shifted a lot of shite, together with a van full of awkwardly-shaped items. We also did a lot of laughing, which certainly helped. We enjoyed a picnic lunch, perching on the back of the van's tailgate. It wasn't exactly fine dining but it was infinitely preferable to eating anywhere inside the house.

It was a long, hard, but productive day. I managed to drive the large van without pranging anything, and even managed to back into the driveway at the Hammer House. That's never easy as there's a steep bank and it's possible to roll a vehicle there if you judge it wrongly. A locum doctor visiting Mother on one occasion almost did exactly that, having to call a tow truck when her car was left balancing precariously on the brink.

We did manage to have a break and some fun on Jill's stay, including lunch out with the person who was translating Sell the Pig into French for me. That was going incredibly well, none of the horrors and disasters of the last time, so I was confident the little Pig might finally make it to the French market.

We had a second assault on the house later in the week, when we'd recovered, and we managed to completely clear the top storey of all the shite. It was encouraging because it meant there was at least one part of the house to show to potential buyers, who would surely soon be queuing round the block, to remind them of what the place had been like in its glory days and could be like once more, with just a little bit of TLC.

In between, we walked the dogs, visited the soap factory, talked politics with Domi and chatted about my brother. It all helped the healing.

We finished off Jill's stay with our usual blow-out meal at our favourite restaurant, with Jill kindly treating me to mine. Then, not without a touch of sadness, it was time to take her back to the airport and wave her off once more. She'd been such a huge help and comfort to me, but now I was on my own again – until the next visitors arrived.

Chapter Eleven
The Great Escape

Friends think my passion for going away camping, especially wild camping, is completely mad, and definitely so for a single female in her sixties. I have another habit which everyone, especially the French think is even more bizarre. When I haven't time to get away anywhere, I'm perfectly happy to put up one of my collection of tents in the garden and sleep in it. Like a big kid.

Why on earth would any home owner with a nice cosy cottage decide instead to sleep outside in the garden? I'm often asked. Because I need the connection with nature, with Mother Earth. I'm sure I must have been a traveller in a previous life, or a wild woman of some sort. I just love the thrill of sleeping outdoors whenever I can.

With all that I had going on currently, there was no chance of me getting away, even for one night. I was now going to the Hammer House of Horrors, which I always abbreviated on social media to HHofH, up to three times a week, coming back each time with poor Roo the Kangoo groaning with yet another heavy load. Everything I brought back I stocked in the hayloft of my barn. It all smelt too bad to even contemplate bringing it into the house. What a good job I had had such a blitz on my barn recently and cleared out vast areas of floor space, although it was filling up at an alarming rate.

The HHofH still contained some of my own stuff, which

I'd left behind when I moved out. Then there were all of Mother's things from her house in Stockport, plus everything of my brother's which had been brought out from his house in Wales, and that building was almost as large as the HHofH. That gave a total of eight dining tables, to start with, to give you an idea of the scale of it all.

Add to all of this my brother's collecting habit and you might start to form a picture of what I was up against. Except I bet it will be an underestimate. We could play a guessing game. You know those thin wooden boxes used for fruit and vegetables, especially oranges? How many of those do you think you can stuff into a garage designed for two large cars parked in tandem, with work space down the sides? I can assure you that it's a lot. I lost the will to live trying to count them all.

Why would you want to? Because my brother could never resist driving past any freebie he saw without stopping to pick it up. He was definitely a Womble in a previous life. Or perhaps one of The Borrowers. Those boxes are great for breaking up for kindling, it has to be said, but I've now got probably a year's supply of kindling as I brought them all back with me. Well, I had to clear them out in order to get into the garage and having done so it seemed to make sense to get some use out of them.

Old pallets, are kid? Yes, why not, I could just do with a dozen or so of those. And so it went on. I tried to keep laughing about it because I knew that the moment I didn't laugh, I would just break down and start crying again and I wasn't sure I would be able to stop.

I was getting exhausted with the trips. These days I don't drive much at all and the unaccustomed mileage was taking its toll. Strange sleeping patterns weren't helping, either. I either slept like a dead thing for nine hours straight, or woke up in the middle of the night and couldn't get back to sleep, so I sat up drinking rooibos tea and reading a library book. I thought it was probably understandable, in the circumstances. It was only later I thought I'd better check that my health wasn't doing daft things once more. But more of that anon.

I needed something to help me through what I was dealing with, and particularly my brushes with the Angling Bumateurs of The Madhouse, who had started to show their true colours. They had sent me the promised form to reclaim the funeral expenses. As they'd been paid from one of my brother's bank accounts, it followed, logically, that the reimbursement needed to go into that account to avoid any overdraft. Except that said form required the signature of the account holder. Rather difficult, as it was his funeral the payment was for. I was starting to think he hadn't, after all, been exaggerating, at least not on that score.

So what would be a normal sort of thing for someone in their sixties to do to help themselves through tough times? Have a spa day? Go clothes or shoes shopping? Meet friends for a girlie lunch? How would I know, I don't do normal. My answer was to dig out a tent, put it up in a corner of the garden and sleep in it whenever possible.

I love being in a tent in all weathers, especially during a storm. Unfortunately, Fleur doesn't share my enthusiasm and turns into a shaking, panting, dribbling thing, trying to burrow her way out through the rip-stop nylon. Rosie was more courageous about storms. So whenever uncertain weather was forecast, we had to go back into the house and batten down the hatches, including unplugging telephone line and internet, which were usually the first casualties in an electric storm.

My friends, both in real life and those on social media, shook their heads in despair at Tottie's foolishness. I have a custom-made orthopaedic mattress, which cost over a thousand Euros, on my bed in the house, but I prefer to sleep on the ground outside. Although as I get older, I have awarded myself a nice memory foam camping mattress. Well, I do have two slipped cervical discs and a thoracic wedge fracture, al of which deserve a bit of pampering.

I'd recently decided to sell my big two-bedroomed tent, and the small camping trailer I transported it in. I was getting a bit worried about all the bills I was going to have to pay, and not knowing if there would be anything left for me to inherit at the end of it all. I started scratching round for anything I could sell and those two items topped the list.

I put them on Le Bon Coin, the French equivalent of things like Gumtree in the UK, and quickly got interest in both. A Moroccan man came for the trailer, to take on a family trip back to his native country. We haggled fiercely, in true North African style, and finally shook hands on a price, both clearly thinking we'd got one over on the other and feeling well content with our bargaining skills.

The woman who phoned up to come and look at the tent was so pleased at the price she asked me, twice, if it was correct or if I'd made a mistake. I needed some cash, but at the same time, if I could help someone else out with a bargain, that would make me happy.

I got the tent out of its bag and spread it out on the grass to show her how to put it up, which was quite easy. I'd even done it on my own a few times, although it was always simpler with two people. She'd come with her brother to collect it and told me she had four children and they were soon off on a family holiday at the seaside. She obviously didn't have a lot of money so was thrilled with her purchase. It gave me a lot of pleasure to think that it would be going to a home where it would get plenty of use and make a family happy.

That left me with my small two-man pop-up tent, Loppy Lugs, and the roomy four-man, which often doubled as an outdoor dining room in case of rain, Count Basie. You may well remember, from earlier books my habit of naming all inanimate objects in my entourage. I set up Basie on the only nearly-flat piece of land in the garden and made it cosy for me and the dogs.

We slept in it whenever we could, me loving lying in my nice sleeping bag listening to the sounds of night animals. Hedgehogs would grunt and snuffle as they passed us by. I would have to be careful to watch out for their deposits the next day as Rosie loves nothing more than rolling in hedgehog poo and it is far too pungent to want to share a tent with her afterwards, unless I first wash her in tea tree oil shampoo.

The slight slope of the ground inevitably meant that I would wake up having rolled off the memory foam mattress to be lying on the floor, with two snoring collie dogs occupying my previous comfy spot. Despite that, it was wonderful to be doing what I enjoyed, cooking my meals outdoors on my rocket stove, then sleeping out under the stars. The perfect antidote to the long and difficult days I was facing.

Chapter Twelve
White rabbits x 3

No matter how bad he got, it was rare for the first day of any month to go by without me getting an email or a text from my brother with that old British traditional greeting for luck, 'White rabbits, white rabbits, white rabbits.'

It was something we always did in our family. It clearly doesn't work, however, as we've never been the luckiest family in the world. Some families say 'Pinch, punch, first of the month, no returns.' Maybe we should have tried that one instead. But for us it was always White Rabbits.

Strangely, it was the thing I missed most about my brother. He would email me most days but it was always that one, first thing in the morning on the first day of the month, which seemed somehow touching. It's meant to be the first thing you say for it to work, and it was always the first email of the day I received, from him.

As is often the way with the internet and emails, some gremlin in the works somewhere meant that I would occasionally get an email with my brother's name as the sender. Although I knew it was nonsense, just a case of stolen email addresses, it gave me a nasty jolt the first couple of times it happened. But I did miss those White Rabbits.

I'd taught Domi lots of quaint English sayings and folklore, some of them not ideal for polite company, but they amused her. She loved the White Rabbits tradition, so it was lovely when she took over and I would get a text message from her, the first thing I read when I woke up on the first day of the month. Although in the interests of brevity and text speak, her messages, sent from her early morning postal round, simply said 'White rabbits x 3.'

It was now already four months since my brother had died, and I was approaching my birthday. He'd been telling me for some time that he was in the process of making me a present, something which he hoped I would love. He wouldn't say what it was, he just kept mentioning it, but it had already failed to materialise for one birthday and a Christmas.

He was always good about remembering my birthday, though. I would usually get a card from him, and an email. He'd sometimes try to send me a cheque to get myself a present. Latterly, he'd become pretty much incapable even of filling out a cheque properly, often forgetting to sign it, or making a mistake with the date, or the amount. The intention was always there, but I now had a collection of useless cheques as I seldom had the heart to point out his errors.

I was, though, determined to find this mystery present, even if unfinished, to have something special to remember him by. When firing on all cylinders, he was brilliant at making things, often inventing something from scratch. He'd made me a wonderful, if slightly heavy, solar lantern torch for camping trips, with two extremely bright LED spotlights. It was more than earning its keep while I was clearing out the HHofH as, the electricity bill and many others having remained unpaid, the power had been cut off and there was no lighting to work by.

Another of his brilliant inventions had been a campfire tripod, made out of the frame of an old ironing board. He also liked camping and cook-outs, so he'd put a lot of thought into its construction and it was a stable piece of kit. It was designed to straddle a campfire, with a chain to support a kettle or cooking pot over the flames, plus two grill shelves made from a recycled shopping trolley.

Eventually, I did find something which may possibly have been what he was working on for me. It was a sort of open, three-sided box on castors. It was exactly the right depth for the size of logs I use on my kitchen range, which are some twenty centimetres shorter than the ones he used for his wood-burner. So I decided that was his work-in-progress present to me, an easy to move log storer. It now sits in my kitchen, next to Leo the Lohberger. My firewood fits it exactly, and whenever I need to replenish or move it, it's light and simple to move, rather than having to lug a traditional log basket.

Brilliant, are kid. Thanks for the present.

One thing that's usually guaranteed to cheer me up, no matter how low I feel, is a tea party. I love them! I don't know if it's a particularly northern trait, but it's something we did a lot in the family home. When I was at school, my best friend and I used to visit an elderly woman who lived alone and craved company, and she loved a tea party. She'd been in service as a girl so had high standards. We always had to have paper doilies on the cake plate. I remember her saying what a wonderful tea party we would have when her husband died – it was not a happy marriage. With sad irony, pneumonia took her first, so she missed out.

I love baking and, if I say so myself, I don't make a bad cake. I've had to adjust my baking to fit round my recent dietary restrictions, but I now have a tried and trusted selection of recipes which mean I can usually rustle up something tasty in a comparatively short time for any visitors who need tea and cake.

Current favourite is a one-bowl chocolate cake which is so gooey it's almost sinful. Easy to make, too, with the kind of ingredients often found in fridge and store cupboard. The reason it's so moist is it's made with oil, not butter, with eggs, sour cream and cocoa powder. I serve it with a *ganache* (icing) made from cream and chocolate.

Buying cream is a completely different experience in France to Britain. We don't have anything like the number of different types. No double and single cream, no whipping cream, certainly no clotted cream. In most of the supermarkets the choice is pretty much between pouring cream, varying only by the fat content, usually UHT, and crème fraîche, the thick soured cream beloved of the French.

Neither is ideal for my other stand-by tea party treat, Eton Mess. If you don't know it, it's wonderfully simple to make, with just three ingredients, delicious to eat, and best of all, requires no creative talent at all to put together. You just mash up some strawberries, break up some meringues – bought ones are fine – and chuck both into a bowl of whipped cream. Fabulous!

The cake went down well when a fellow writer stopped by for a quick visit with her husband. We'd met on social media and again once when Alex was visiting. They enjoyed visiting the campsite at nearby Thiers, so had decided to have a run-out into the wilds to come and visit me and meet the dogs.

However the Eton Mess turned into a bit of a disaster when Laura, Ashes Transporter Extraordinaire, came with her husband and daughter. I'd made the mistake of buying a different brand of cream to that which I usually used. When I started to whip it, it very quickly tried to transform itself into butter which was not the idea at all. It produced something strange to look at, which luckily tasted good. As neither the husband nor the daughter had had it before, they didn't know the difference, and Laura kindly kept the secret.

When I later studied the carton the cream had come in, during a post tea party inquest into the disaster, I discovered that it had carrageen in it. Why, I have no idea, but I have made myself a mental note not to buy the same brand again.

It was wonderful to meet Laura in the flesh finally and we seemed to make a connection. It was a nice day for their visit so we were able to sit outside in the garden and enjoy the views and the *craic*, as the Irish say.

Fleur has always loved visitors. When it comes to people, she loves everyone unreservedly. She's never met a person she doesn't like. Rosie is still nervous of anyone new, but she is getting braver and even allowed herself to be stroked by Laura and her daughter, though she still draws the line at letting strange men touch her.

Rosie had more challenges to cope with when a good social media friend of mine, Emma, came to stay, complete with her small son and her mum, whom I'd also met online. Emma is one of my team of beta-readers, those essential second eyes over what I write. Particularly with the crime fiction, it's so easy to overlook plot holes unless the betas have a read through of everything before it goes to print.

Four people is too much of a squeeze in my small grottage, but as I had my tent up in the garden anyway, the dogs and I slept in there and let our visitors have my room and the guest room. The stay was brief but enjoyed by all and Rosie even got brave enough to allow Small Son to stroke her.

I'd decided to have a tea party for my birthday, which was to be at a weekend, three days after the actual date, to suit my young former English students, back on holiday from their universities, with social diaries as full as only young people's seem to be. On the actual day of my birthday itself, my friends Geoff and Christine, who live not all that far away, suggested we meet somewhere for a coffee, to mark the occasion. As it's fairly convenient for both of us, we opted to meet in Southampton.

No, not really! We weren't planning on going back to the UK just for a couple of hours. Southampton had become a standing joke between me and my former handyman, Patrick, because he couldn't pronounce the word when his daughter flew there on a visit to England and I initially had trouble pronouncing the local small town Cunlhat, which the locals turn into something a bit like Cuh-yah, although it varies. So I often to refer to Cunlhat as Southampton.

The tea party at the weekend was great fun. A dear friend through Facebook, Kay, the person I call my soul sister, who lives in Wales, sent me a mystery parcel for my birthday, which turned out to contain pretty party bunting and an elegant mini candelabra for the cake.

The weather couldn't quite make up its mind, but we managed to spend some time outdoors, although to avoid disasters, I put up the bunting and served up the cake indoors.

Before my guests arrived – Domi, Muta, plus my two ladies and two girls, as I always call them, but I should now call them young ladies, from the old English group – I had what I can only describe as a First World crisis. I scalded my *ganache*. Not a euphemism for some intimate medical emergency, I just overheated the cream to which I would add chunks of chocolate to make a thick, shiny, rich icing for the cake.

When I caught myself bemoaning this supposed disaster on social media, I gave myself a stern talking to. 'There are people with no homes and no food and you're moaning about scalded *ganache*? Seriously, Tottie, get over yourself, silly self-indulgent tart.'

Chapter Thirteen
Seventy-six trombones...

..led the big parade. So goes the song. If, like me, you are afflicted by earworms, those tunes which implant themselves in your brain for hours at a time, usually triggered by a word you hear, you're now stuck humming that for the rest of the day. Sorry!

Mine is an extension of word association. Football. You see? One word immediately brings another to mind, like Association Football, and that will then provoke the inevitable earworm. In case you're interested, I now have the song 'Football Crazy' from Scottish folk duo Robin Hall and Jimmie Macgregor, playing on a repeating loop in my head, and likely to be so for the rest of the day. And people wonder why I'm crazy.

Some of my brother's impulse buys were going to be interesting to dispose of, and I'm not just talking about a London Routemaster bus. Ting, ting. His method was – See, Buy, Remove from package, Fail to read instructions, Break, Cast aside, Buy another.

He was always musical. The piano was his main instrument and he had one of those at the HHofH. A good make, brought over from the UK, but like everything else in the house, not having been greatly enhanced by a selection of stray cats peeing on it. It also hadn't been tuned in years and when someone had come to give an estimate to do so, my brother had

had his usual meltdown at being told it was not good for a wooden-framed piano to be in a room with fluctuating temperatures, caused by his constant battles with his wood-burner.

There was also a trombone in a rigid case. It looked hardly used but there was some oxidisation on the rim and one of the catches on the case, so it had clearly been wet at some time. Hopefully it had been a victim of the flood, rather than of the cats. He'd had one back in Wales, a much better quality one. I had no idea where that had ended up. It was probably still on the furniture lorry, parked up in Hereford.

There was also a fancy electronic keyboard/synthesiser sort of thing. To me it looked like the control panel on the Star Ship Enterprise and I doubted I would even be able to turn it on and off. But it had cost a lot of money so I lugged it back to the grottage for future cleaning up and possibly selling online.

There were all sorts of techie gadgets, including some clever thing which somehow converted a TV into a computer, or something like that, according to what I read about it. There were four of those, all identical. I never got any of them to work, nor did a much more technically-minded friend who came round to see if he could help. Goodness knows what my brother had done to them.

Hidden away behind years of detritus in the garage was a lovely old thing which had once been his pride and joy but had lain untouched in ten years. A pianola. Also known as a player piano, it was a marvellous party trick; a piano which played itself. It could be used as an ordinary piano but, throw a switch, open sliding doors in the front and insert a parchment role with holes in it, pedal away rhythmically on the big, wide pedals, rather like those on an organ, and it would play all by itself.

Ten years of neglect inevitably meant that not only was it in serious need of retuning but the rubber tubes which carried air to make the mechanism work, although I have no real idea of how it does, had been chewed to holes by countless rodents.

The whole thing needed a serious tuning and overhaul as, despite throwing all the levers I could find, I couldn't get any sound out of it in pianola mode, although the keyboard played, not very tunefully.

When I pedalled enthusiastically, the roll went round, but the brass needle which 'read' the holes and converted them into music didn't seem to do its stuff. It didn't help that it was right at the back of the garage, the darkest part, and I knew from previous experience of trying to shift it that it was extremely heavy. It would be difficult to manoeuvre into a lighter part to see if there was something simple which would make it work once more.

I knew that, once restored, it was worth thousands. I'd seen the same make and model, back in showroom condition, on an American site for sale for more than twenty thousand. But in its present state I had no idea of its value nor of its retail potential. But I knew a man who might.

My brother had had the estimate done to retune the ordinary piano, but, as well as taking umbrage at the advice, he'd then hadn't wanted to pay what he was quoted, so he'd left it. I knew that the firm who had done the estimate sometimes bought and sold second-hand instruments so I contacted them.

They were kind and helpful but their response was disappointing. They weren't interested in the piano for several reasons. Because it was wooden-framed, it was a devil to keep in tune, reacting as it did to any change in ambient temperature or humidity. It was also an English make, little known in France, so not at all sought after.

That was to turn out to be a recurring theme for all the family treasures I was uncovering. Some of them were valuable, like a beautiful nineteenth century rare Wedgwood Blue Harlequin Ariel pattern breakfast service. But there was no demand for anything like that out here in rural France, and the risks involved in packaging it up to post anywhere, if I put it on eBay, were too great.

We'd always used that service for breakfast with friends after church on Sundays. It was part of my heritage. I couldn't bear the idea of it getting bashed about and damaged in transit.

I asked the helpful man at the piano shop if he knew anything about the pianola and in particular where I could find someone who could tune it and have a look at it with a view to a realistic valuation. More disappointing news. He said they no longer had anyone with the ability to tune such a specialist instrument and he could tell me with certainty that there was no one in all of central France who still had the skills to do so. He did make a helpful suggestion on the likely market value of the piano, but that was as far as it went.

In theory, it was the executor of the estate who should be dealing with the disposal of the assets. But that was Mr Wales, in whom I had already lost all faith, so I started on the task myself. Just as well, as he didn't seem to have a clue as to where or how to begin. I thought I'd start with the bus, as I knew there was a market for those amongst collectors.

I started by making contact with the Routemaster Association. They told me it was worth a lot of money fully restored. Where had I heard that before? As it stood, it had no tax, insurance or test certificate, had been parked outside for ten years and not driven in about five. One of their members, who dealt in them, offered to go and see it and value it for me, but wanted paying up front for his time and travel.

Fair enough, but as with everything else, I was short of the funds to do any speculating to accumulate. I explained that I was after a quick sale at a low figure just to be rid of it and to stop it incurring any more storage costs. I knew what my brother had paid for it and I knew how to use keywords to dangle the carrot of a Routemaster in front of the noses of those likely to be interested.

Before long, I had a fish on the end of my hook. He said he'd go along, at his own expense, to have a look, take some pictures of it so I could see for myself the condition it was in and, if he was interested, he would make me a genuine offer.

He was certainly full of it. He said he ran a bus hire company in London, hiring them out for all sorts of things like proms, weddings, tourist trips. All his buses had a name, he told me, and he would name this one Peter after my brother when it was restored and put back in service. It would also be going back to its old stamping ground, the West End.

All very impressive. He didn't, however, know he was talking to a journalist, albeit retired, and former investigative reporter. I'd already looked him up and knew everything about him that was available in the public domain, with just a bit of digging, including his criminal record. I knew he had several different companies and thanks to Google Street View, I'd even had a look at all of the premises where he had addresses.

He went to visit, sent me the promised photos and made me an offer under what I was asking. The poor old bus did look in a sorry state. It had been a thing of some beauty and elegance in its time. Now it was stained and scruffy, with bits missing. I could have got more, but it would have been difficult to organise the repairs and everything else from a distance and I no longer travel, certainly not back to the UK.

I decided a bird in the hand was definitely worth more than no matter how many in the bush in this case. It would be one more thing off my mind, especially with storage charges mounting all the time it remained there.

I sent strict idiot-proof instructions to Mr Wales that he was in no circumstances to release the duplicate log book or a receipt for the bus until the money had arrived in his account, as he was the executor, and had remained there for long enough not to bounce.

Peter the bus went off back up to London on a tow truck. I never heard another word from Mr 'I'll keep in touch and let you know when it's back in service.'

No surprises there, then.

Once those who had previously been sniffing around but wanted paying to go and look at it got wind of what it had sold for, I got various grumpy emails saying they would have paid more. One even said they would have paid half as much again.

All of which just goes to show that in the world of selling buses, like everything else, he who hesitates is lost.

Chapter Fourteen
Him, Daniel Blake

My brother always wanted to do good. To help those who had less than he did. Which, these days, amounted to a large part of the population. If there is a hell, and if he should have finished up there, he will feel at home as, apparently, the road there is paved with good intentions, and he had plenty of those. Few of them ever came to fruition, sadly.

He would tell me sometimes, in endless emails, that watching those television appeals – you know the sort of thing, donate X pounds a month and provide clean drinking water for half the planet, or whatever it is they claim – could reduce him to tears.

The trouble was, he never seemed able to go from there to taking the fairly simple steps to make the donation. Then the fact that he had not done so would make him cry some more and become depressed, and so it would go on.

He sent me one of his long, rambling emails about watching an old man in a supermarket putting his purchases on the check-out belt and being saddened by how meagre they were. He said he wanted to offer to pay for them and to urge the man to buy more. But his usual reticence and inability to interact held him back.

The film most people were talking about in 2016 was *I, Daniel Blake*, Ken Loach's work about the dreadful effect of benefit sanctions on those already in dire straits. As well as working our way through my crime fiction books when she comes for her English lessons, my friend Domi and I enjoy discussing politics and world affairs.

France has been going through some degree of austerity of late, though nothing like on a par with that which has been sweeping the British Isles. Here, the old age pension is quite generous, for example. Britain's is one of the worst in Europe, a mere pittance by comparison, although the age of entitlement has been steadily creeping up in both countries. I'll probably live to see younger people have to work into their seventies to qualify for any pension at all.

The whole concept of benefit sanctions has not yet caught hold in France. Sometimes when I give Domi examples of the harshness, I sense she thinks something is getting lost in the translation. She knows I wouldn't deliberately make such things up.

I tell her about the man who was sanctioned for failing to complete his compulsory interview to review his benefits. I wonder if she thinks it's some strange British joke when I tell her the reason he didn't complete it was that he had the audacity to suffer a heart attack during the interview.

Or the man who was sanctioned for not replying to a letter he received from the Department of Work and Pensions instructing him to contact them. Only the reason he didn't reply was because his disability had left him blind and he couldn't read the letter. And so the sorry saga went on.

Through the wonderful world of Twitter, I came across someone who was going through his own personal Daniel Blake moment and it saddened me enormously that there was little I could do to help. I sent platitudes of support, which were well received, but I wanted to do more. I asked him what I could usefully do, from France, to make a difference and he suggested I make a donation to the Trussell Trust.

They have a network of some 400 foodbanks in Britain. I had just had the first sniff of a possibility of selling something of my brother's, the trombone, so I thought it would be nice to donate the money from that to the Trust, in his memory. If there was anything else I could spare, I would do something for a similar charity in France, but having made personal contact with someone in the UK, I wanted to do something there first.

I don't like to count my chickens. I know I'm optimistic but I can also be cautious. It did look very hopeful, though, that the trombone would be sold, and to a good home.

When someone contacted me via Le Bon Coin about my advert and said they were from outside the area, I tried to put them off. They would need to see the instrument before buying it, I told them, as I know nothing about them, have never played one, so couldn't comment on whether or not it was a good one. A friend of my friend Jilli, in Italy, does know a fair bit about them and had been able to value it for me from some photos and the model number, but that was as far as it went.

The woman who was interested went so far as to phone me up to ask about it. She was well spoken and sounded quite sensible. She assured me that it was just what she was looking for and the price was reasonable, much less than she would expect to pay further south in a smarter, more expensive area of France where she lived. Her family were clubbing together to buy one for her as she had just started having lessons, so the price was well within the budget they had set between them. The slight problem was that she didn't have a car so she was looking into the costs of rail travel to come and collect it.

This was all starting to sound very strange. I would have thought she could have bought the entire brass section of a small, local village band for what it was likely to cost her to come up by train to collect the trombone. She clearly thought the same thing as she then sent me a text to say could I tell her the weight of it, in its case, and she would make enquiries with La Poste about how much it would be to send it via parcel post.

At least a trombone was possibly not quite such a strange item to send by mail as an urn of ashes had been, but I was starting to think this was all getting into the realms of fantasy.

I replied to her text with the weight and added a note that I was donating the amount received to help the homeless, as my brother would have wished. This brought an even more enthusiastic text back from her saying she was so pleased to be able to contribute something for such a good cause, and especially in memory of my late brother.

Fired up by her enthusiasm, I went online and made the donation to the Trussell Trust. Of course, by the next day, the would-be buyer had gone off the whole thing and decided it was all too much of an effort.

Oh well. It wasn't a huge amount. I could stand the hit – just – although it was alarming how many bills I was suddenly having to pay from my meagre income. I'd already had to fork out two lots of *taxe foncière*, a land tax, roughly the equivalent of property tax in the UK, on my own and my brother's houses. His being so much bigger than mine, it was nearly twice as much as mine but, me being the sole heir, it was down to me to pay it and any delay would attract hefty interest, not to mention bailiffs' letters..

Some critics of *I, Daniel Blake* say it's exaggerated left-wing propaganda and life isn't really like that. I actually know, through social media, people who are using foodbanks because of genuine need. It saddens me to think that in the twenty-first century, in a supposedly civilised country like Britain, people are going hungry and children are going to school with not enough food in their stomachs.

I'd just have to advertise the trombone again and hope to find a genuine buyer the next time. In the meantime there were other possessions which I didn't want to keep which could be sold on. There was, for one thing, a furniture lorry, in the same off-road storage as the bus had been, which needed to be disposed of. Knowing my brother, it was probably stuffed to the gunwales with all sorts of things which most people would undoubtedly call rubbish but he clung on to for some sentimental reason. No doubt there was personal stuff amongst it all, but I would have to let the lorry go for scrap and it was not worth the time or effort to get someone to go and clear it for me.

There were a lot of things amongst his impulse buys which would come in handy for me, which was some small consolation. I'd found a television which worked, among many which didn't, and it was a nicer size and better make than my current one. There was also a DVD player of a much more recent vintage than mine, plus lots of unopened DVDs which I would enjoy watching. They gave me my introduction to the Wallender crime series, amongst other things.

I'd been thinking of replacing the old wooden floor in my sitting room when I had the funds to do it. The floorboards are nice, big, old oak planks, but not tongue and grooved. They've warped over the years so there are gaps which let through quite a draft from the cellar underneath, despite my best efforts at insulating. I found enough good quality floor tiles, of an ideal colour, Italian made, plus the boards to lay them on, to cover the entire room. My brother had bought them for some scheme or another, possibly for the back room in the cellar which he seemed to have been thinking of turning into some sort of music studio, despite it being dark and damp.

Then there was the bulk buying. Three brand new showers. I could advertise those online as they'd never been installed. Enough cleaning products to have kept the HHofH sparkling for years, if only he or his 'cleaner' had opened some of them. It's likely that by the time I run out of them, I will be too old and senile to be thinking of cleaning my own home.

And don't get me started on tinned fish. I do eat fish, occasionally, fortunately, as I uncovered enough for about a year's supply, and that's after I'd given away tons of it to a food bank collection point here in France. Although I don't take much notice of 'sell by' dates on tinned goods, any which did look at all elderly or suspect would be gratefully received by the dogs and the cats.

Some of the electronic gadgets and power tools I couldn't even begin to define the purpose of. I just brought everything back and stored it where I could in my barn, to be looked at and evaluated as and when I could. Even with his catastrophic record of breaking things, there had to be some items amongst it all which still worked.

The pressing need first was to present the house as empty and as clean as I could possibly make it, for if and when people started to want to view it. I just hoped it would be soon. It was a financial and emotional burden which I didn't need, and with winter coming on, there was the worry of it deteriorating if left empty. Not to mention me having to make that journey on snow-covered roads, with the real risk of deep drifts to battle through, as the HHofH was high up and exposed.

I needed rid, and soon.

Chapter Fifteen
I believe in Father Christmas

It's another earworm. A song from Greg Lake, of Emerson, Lake and Palmer. He'd died just as I was writing this part of the book so it was getting a lot of airtime. A sad and rather cynical song about the supposed magic and miracles of Christmas.

I certainly don't believe in miracles, although I could have done with a few about now. In particular, I could have done with a grown up to come and take over everything. I wasn't feeling up to a lot of it myself and I was only just starting out on a long and protracted process. I needed to find my big girl pants, pull them up, and ride into battle. I would have preferred to stay in my blanket fort with my colouring books and crayons.

But then, perhaps there are miracles. Perhaps the stars were just in the right alignment, or whatever it is you happen to believe in. Because one day in August, just five months after my brother's death, I got a phone call.

A polite woman's voice apologised for contacting me unsolicited but said she was a neighbour of the mayor of my brother's commune. She had a large family and several dogs and they were looking to move to a bigger house. She had heard, through the mayor, that my brother's place might be on the market and could they possibly have a look at it?

I tried to keep the excitement out of my voice. Above all,

not to do a loud squeeee down the phone. I hadn't even put the house on the market yet and here was a potential buyer already. A private sale, direct between individuals, would save a fortune in agents' fees and could potentially go through much more quickly. It's what I'd done when I bought my grottage. It meant I could ask an attractive price for a quick sale, without adding agents' fees on top.

It certainly sounded like a miracle in the making. Knowing my luck, it also sounded too good to be true, so I tried not to get my hopes up and to play it cool.

I stifled a giggle while typing that as I immediately thought of the immortal scene in the television show *Only Fools and Horses,* when Del Boy and Trig (David Jason and Roger Lloyd-Pack) are out on the pull in a pub. Not a show I ever watched much nor greatly enjoyed, but that brief scene remains a classic comedy moment. If you don't know it, you'll easily find it on YouTube.

'Play it nice and cool, son. Nice and cool.'

I warned the potential buyers of the state the house was in. I was perfectly candid about it. I didn't want to be wasting either their time or mine. We made an appointment to meet at the house on a Friday afternoon so that I could show them round.

It has to be said that I didn't altogether trust *Monsieur le Maire,* who had put them in touch with me. Mayors hold enormous power here in France, especially in the small rural communes. I'd already heard him talking to Domi on our first visit to the HHofH and expressing an opinion on the house's value, which I hadn't found altogether professional. I didn't much like the idea of him knowing so much about my or my brother's private business, but that's the way of life here so there was nothing I could do except to accept it.

The potential buyers arrived promptly for the viewing, which was good. They also arrived with the mayor, which I was not so thrilled about, especially as he had brought along a woman who was presumably his wife or at least Significant Other.

It's a peculiarity around here that people don't always introduce themselves to you when you meet for the first time so I was not introduced to the Plus One. I suspected she and the mayor were just there to have a good old nosy around the legendary house and I didn't much like that. It felt like a lack of respect to my brother.

I didn't want to start out by making waves, though. Genuine buyers were as rare as hen's teeth in these difficult times so I was keen to avoid anything which might rock the boat. I wanted to sell. I was desperate to sell. The house just felt like a massive millstone around my neck and was already costing me money as I'd had to take over paying insurance on it, not to mention settling all the outstanding utility bills.

The buyers turned out to be a couple who looked to be in their forties. The wife told me they had four children, hence the need for plenty of bedrooms. Despite having to cover their noses, as the smell had still not entirely gone, I could tell they were interested. Very much so, although playing it as cool as Del Boy and Trig. Most promising of all for me was that they said they were perfectly happy to clear it themselves of anything I couldn't manage to move.

I could almost hear my brother's voice in my ear as they said it.

'If a thing sounds too good to be true, it usually is.'

There may be trouble ahead. But for now, they admitted to being interested and, naturally enough, wanted to know the asking price. I promised to look carefully at the estate agents' estimates, crunch a few numbers, and come back to them as soon as possible.

We were, by this time, back outdoors where it was more fragrant, although it did look like the worst kind of illegal travellers' site, with all the rubbish lying about.

Mr Potential Buyer's eyes fell on the old motorhome,

parked up in a corner, the one my brother had bought in order to transport our frail, elderly mother out to France when we had first moved in 2007. Like everything else of my brother's, it had been a lovely thing in its heyday but was now in a sorry state. It was a Hymer motorhome on a Fiat Ducato chassis, with sleeping for five, a shower, kitchen, plenty of fitted cupboards. Ideal for a big family.

Or at least it had been. Now it was scruffy and stuffed full of junk. It looked as if someone had tried to hot-wire it, as there were cables trailing everywhere around the dashboard and steering column. The roof above the Luton leaked and I lacked the courage to open the door of the shower room, dreading what I might find within. The fitted wardrobe and cupboards contained another couple of dozen shirts, amongst other things, as well as yet more unwrapped brand new underwear and socks. I knew socks were always well received in clothing banks as they tended to be things that people forget to donate. The local homeless were going to be having much warmer feet of late, thanks to my brother's shopping addiction.

I knew the motorhome was currently under a statutory off-road notice because my brother had been stopped for driving with a defective brake light. He was always careful not to drive if he had been drinking and despite being stopped and booked several times for minor infringements, he had never been found to be over the limit. Perhaps there really are miracles.

The motorhome was yet another of the headaches facing me. Without the magic *controle technique*, certificate of road-worthiness, I couldn't even advertise it for sale, let alone sell it. The laws here are strict on such things. There was also the little electric Clio, the one my brother and our friend Young Bobby had driven halfway round France to collect. That had had an intermittent fault since he'd first bought it which meant that the motor was prone to cutting out without warning. Again, it was going to be a costly business to get it through its test to get the certificate.

I just wanted rid of both, as soon as possible. More in hope than anticipation, I asked if Mr Potential Buyer was interested. When he said he might be, I offered to throw both vehicles in free if we could agree on a price for the house and he was prepared to accept them, too, as they stood.

I needed as much as I could get from the sale. Unpaid bills were continuing to pile up at an alarming rate in my brother's letterbox. Despite having the means, he had always been bad about paying them. He would never pay on the first bill, nor on the first reminder. He would usually wait for the letter of warning from the bailiffs, a letter written on green paper here, before he started to take things seriously. That meant that he'd died without dealing with several of them, as his death was so sudden.

All of these would have to be paid out of his estate, so I had a duty, as well as a vested interest, to try to get as much as possible from the sale of his assets. But the caveat was the same as for the bus. It was already costing me money for the house to stand empty, and its value would only go down the longer it remained so. In addition, a monumental referendum decision in June for Britain to leave the European Union risked killing the possibility of a sale to anyone from the UK planning to move to France, at least until anyone knew what the heck was going to happen. Meanwhile, the pound was in free-fall, making it even harder to sell to the British market.

Birds and bushes and hands. Those were my watchwords. It was also impossible to put a price on peace of mind. The longer things dragged on, the higher my stress levels were likely to rise. I was already having to take the occasional sleeping tablet to stop myself waking up in the wee small hours with my heart racing and my brain swirling with thoughts which were beyond my comprehension.

I plucked up my courage to phone my potential buyers, gave them a price and told them it was my one and only, take it or leave it, no-haggle price. I held my breath, crossed every limb and digit I could and waited.

They would, they said, be pleased to take it.

I was very restrained. I played it cool, son. Played it nice and cool. Not a single squeee, nor a victory dance, until after I had thanked them politely and hung up. Then the dogs thought I had definitely finally lost the plot as I squeaked loudly while capering stiffly around the kitchen then out into the garden in a sort of victory jig.

I kept reminding myself about slips and cups and lips, and that nothing was over until the fat lady had sung. In our case, nothing was definite until there was a signature on at least a draft contract. But it was a start, and a very good one. An amazing one, all things considered.

The would-be buyers had asked if they could come again in a couple of weeks with someone who was going to cost up essential works for them to make the house habitable. They had a house to sell, they told me, but they wanted to buy the HHofH as soon as possible so they were applying for a loan and wanted also to cover the costs of any work to be done within the amount of the loan. For that they would, of course, need estimates early on, to present their loan application to their bank. I suspect I was as anxious as they were for it all to go through smoothly.

I was happy to oblige. I was happy to do anything at all which would advance things and get the HHofH off my hands as soon as possible.

But first I needed to double check with the Three Soliciteers that it was actually going to be possible to sell the house before the grant of probate in either country. As it stood, it was technically not yet mine to sell.

Chapter Sixteen
Ticked off

The unusually wet spring of 2016 had been followed by a long, hot summer. So much rain had been good news for some things, like a good grass crop, leading to plenty of hay and silage being brought in, to tide the animals over through the long, often harsh, winter months.

This is a largely small-scale agricultural region, mostly cattle. There are lots of herds of the striking red Salers cows in the neighbouring fields, and some Charolais beef cattle. But the cows are predominantly dual-purpose breeds, which the Salers are, like the Aubrac, with colouring similar to Jerseys, and the red and white Monbéliarde. Cattle often wear bells on collars here and it's a soothing sound to hear them clanging away peacefully. Not quite so restful when they put them on young heifers who like to have a mad gallop about their fields occasionally.

Long, lush grass and a wet spring may be good for the farming community, but it was bad news for my arch-enemies – ticks! I've lost count of the number of 'this repellent never fails' remedies I've tried, both on me and on the dogs. I can tell you with some degree of authority that none of them is effective on our little blighters here. We have at least three different species, each as determined as the next, and lots of each. Apparently the Auvergne is one of the areas of France most affected by the dreaded Lyme disease, and around twenty per cent of our ticks are carriers of it.

I'd stepped up a gear for protecting the dogs. I'd abandoned all hope of keeping ticks off them and instead starting using a systemic tablet which killed ticks when they bit. These pills were quite large, round, squishy and with the look and smell of a dog treat. Certainly both Rosie and Fleur had no objection to eating them and so far, they had been the most successful weapon in my armoury. The disadvantage, because of course there is always one, was that they were expensive.

I was tempted to try them myself as, although they didn't stop ticks from attaching themselves, they did appear to give them a short enough life expectancy to drastically reduce the risks of their hosts getting any tick-borne diseases.

But after every walk, especially where there was long grass, there was always the ritual to be gone through, for all three of us, me included. I would have to carefully inspect every inch of our bodies and remove any ticks which had attached themselves with my trusty specially designed tick hook, which went everywhere with me during the high risk times of year. I took precautions for myself, such as always stuffing my trousers into my socks before venturing into the woods. Not exactly a glamorous look, but worth it to reduce the risk as much as I could.

Naturally, I have to remove my glasses in the shower, and I don't see brilliantly without them, which made tick spotting slightly more difficult. One day as I was drying myself, I noticed something unfamiliar, so reached for my specs. As I feared. One of the little buggers had attached itself to the soft flesh on the inside of my thigh, high up.

I carefully twisted it off with the special hook, which is designed to make sure the jaws come away with the body, to reduce the risk of infection. I flushed it triumphantly down the loo then gave the bite area a good clean-up with an antiseptic wash.

I'd lost track of the number of tick bites I've had over the years of living here. It was one of the hazards of enjoying country walks and camping. I thought no more about this one than I had about any of its predecessors.

Then the area where it had bitten me started to itch and become inflamed. Nothing large or dramatic, but there was definitely a characteristic bullseye ring starting to form around the bite, and of all the previous tick attacks I'd had, none had ever reacted like that. And that's a symptom of Lyme disease. Time to get it looked at. Only it wasn't quite that simple.

Kind friends on social media were asking anxiously if I had any other symptoms of Lyme disease, other than the appearance of the ring around the bite. It's true to say that I was tired. Absolutely and utterly knackered, to put it mildly. As tired as I had been before my Silly Coeliac was diagnosed. I'd tended to put it down to all that I had going on, and in no small measure to the amount of driving I was having to do, which was not normal for me.

We were coming up to a long weekend, with a Bank Holiday Monday looming. France is, and has long been, a secular country. That doesn't stop it marking such occasions as the Feast of the Assumption with a national holiday.

On the Friday before the weekend, I'd been back to the HHofH again to let the potential buyers inside with their builder/handyman who was going to cost the work for them. He turned out to be the brother of Mr Potential Buyer. Nothing like keeping it in the family.

I trotted round behind them as they went from room to room discussing their plans for what had, for four years, been my home. Mrs Potential Buyer was clearly in charge of plans, and it sounded as if she was serious in wanting to buy, judging by the ideas she was coming out with. All very encouraging so far.

What had been my bedroom was going to become an extension of the sitting room and, at my suggestion, Madame decided she wanted to open it out onto the garden to the east to make a morning terrace for enjoying the early sun.

They also had big ideas to install a swimming pool on the piece of land down below the fruit trees and vegetable garden, the one I'd always called Meic's Meadow. It was where I exercised my dogs, Meic to start with, then later Ci, when I couldn't go far because of looking after my mother. I could use the baby monitor to listen out for her when I popped down there for a change of scene for both of us. A lively game of doggy football was a great way for both of us to expend a bit of energy and have some fun.

The trip over for this second viewing had wiped me out even more than usual. Clearly something was not right with my system, and I would need to get it sorted. Most unusually for me, I was having to take to my bed during the daytime and sleep, and that was after having slept for about nine hours at night.

Luckily for me, despite being as lively and as mad as a lot of border collies are, both Rosie and Fleur are proper bed-heads, given half the chance. They love snuggling up with me and will always sleep on the bed on all but the hottest of nights. As long as they got chance to go in the garden to relieve themselves and race round after a ball for a few minutes, they were quite happy to join me and sleep, day or night.

I'd phoned up to get an appointment with my own doctor after the bank holiday but unfortunately, she was away on holiday. It was, after all, the height of the holiday season and, in France, people take holidays seriously. She had a stand-in, of course, who was covering her cases from his own surgery in the next small town, but he didn't have a free appointment until later in the week and only at an ungodly hour in the morning.

These days, I'm not much of a morning person. My time of getting up at sparrows' fart to look after horses is long behind me. I'd have struggled to get up for that time even when feeling on top form. As tired as I was, even the thought of it was beyond me.

I would have to make my first ever visit, for myself, to the local hospital Accident and Emergency department, at Thiers. Hospital waiting times here were slowly creeping up of late, though still nothing like as bad as they'd been in the UK when I'd left ten years ago.

I opted to go around lunchtime knowing that, even sick or injured, French people did like their lunch, so I hoped it would be a bit quieter. Total time in A&E including waiting and consultation? Less than fifteen minutes.

The characteristic ring around my bite was still there though still not hugely impressive. The doctor didn't even waste time asking for blood tests to see if I was at risk from Lyme disease. He just treated pro-actively to stop it developing, if I had been infected. Eight days of oral antibiotics, a topical antibiotic cream for applying three times a day until the bite died down and the ring disappeared and some vitamin B tablets to help with the fatigue. French medication tends to go in multiples of eight, rather than seven as in the UK. I had pills for eight days. Fleur is currently taking some for an as yet undiagnosed dizzy spell she had and hers are for twenty-four days.

I was still putting my trousers back on when the doctor wandered off to write the prescription and leave it at reception for me to collect. Of course, this being France, you didn't just get the pills and the cream. As I discovered from my experience of scalding myself previously, you were also issued with everything you needed to treat and dress the wound yourself.

I headed to my local *pharmacie* and came away with a bagful of goodies – more antiseptic solution, some strong stuff to wash the wound in, paraffin gauze to cover it with and special squashy foam sticking plasters to cover it up with. With that amount of kit, I was confident that any bugs the tick had left behind him didn't stand a chance.

I was still sleeping for France in the European Sleeping

Championships and didn't have enough energy to do anything useful, other than at plodding pace. But slowly, as the antibiotics did their stuff, both internally and externally, we went from a definite advantage Mr Tick to Game, Set and Match to Tottie.

Chapter Seventeen
We dig, dig, dig

Not in the mines of Snow White's dwarves, but there was going to be a lot of digging and a lot of haggling at the HHofH in the days and weeks to come.

Many people who visited France in their childhood may retain less than fond memories of the drains. It's true that French plumbing always was different to that found in Britain. Many small towns, if they have a public lavatory at all, still have the dreaded 'Turkish crapper', set into the floor. I once had to drive a visitor all round the outskirts of Clermont-Ferrand to find a 'proper' loo. In the end, in desperation, I took her to a McDonald's. Not somewhere I would usually frequent except for the odd coffee and use of their facilities.

These hole in the floor loos no longer bother me in the least. Nowadays they are generally clean and smell no worse than an ordinary one. And once you master the art of using them, and remember to step well back before you pull the chain, they're just another aspect of French life.

You learn to be less fussy and more resourceful in a country where public loos can be scarce, especially in rural areas. I even managed to use a urinal recently when I found the only cubicle was closed up for winter. Most public toilets here are unisex. Luckily there was no one else in at the time, and I will leave it to your imagination as to how I managed.

Plumbing and waste disposal in rural French homes in

particular has always been a bit haphazard. In that respect, no different to Britain. In fact I would go so far as to say that my septic tank in the UK was worse than a French one as the water discharged into a stream. Which is precisely the reason why you should never drink from streams when out walking in the country, unless you are safely miles away from any habitation.

Worse still, this particular stream at my grottage in Lincolnshire was the home of a famous 'rag well', Lud's Well, where people would leave strips of cloth tied to an old yew tree to bring healing and blessings on loved ones. All of which involved paddling around in said stream. The one where... I won't join up the dots for you. It was famous worldwide, too. The footpath which led to it went past the bottom of the garden of my grottage, not far from Market Rasen, and people would often stop to ask me how to get to the well. One young man had come from Russia and had it on his 'to see' list. Fancy travelling all that way to paddle in the run-off from someone's septic tank.

France's reputation for its smelly drains and septic tanks was undergoing something of a transformation. Since 2012, households have been gradually having to update their private sewerage disposal systems to modern and stringent standards, where no mains drainage is available. It's why I'd had to install an expensive *micro-station d'épuration*, a mini sewage treatment works, in the garden of the grottage. I had bought the house with no form of drainage at all and tried never to dwell on how the former owner had managed without.

The Pink House, as we'd called my brother's house when we bought it, had been built at the end of the 1970s but, although its system was no longer up to modern standards, it had worked well ever since. We'd never needed to get the tank emptied and we'd not had any problems with leakage, smells or anything else undesirable.

The good news for me was that the cost of installing a new system fell to the purchaser, not the vendor, although clearly the seller had to disclose everything they knew about the existing system. Which in my case was not a lot.

Understandably, the potential buyers wanted to know all about it, starting with its location. And with that, I couldn't help them. My brother and I had looked for it on several occasions. I'd even got out my copper dowsing rods and had a go at divining for it, as I've had some success doing that in the past. I did find roughly where the pipes went, but simple logic alone would have found those. The whereabouts of the actual septic tank remained a mystery. There were some pipes which looked like stench pipes sticking out of the ground at the top of the slope behind the house, outside what had been my mother's bedroom. But as that was higher up than any of the lavatories, it didn't make a lot of sense for that to be the location of the septic tank. They may just have been there to ventilate the back cellar rooms.

Although I wouldn't have to pay for the new installation, I did have to pay for the Water and Sanitation Authority to come out and write out a certificate to say that the installation was not up to standard. Exactly the same certificate my brother had had to have done just over three years ago, a copy of which I could no doubt have found somewhere if I'd looked hard enough. Except the certificate is valid for exactly three years only so I would have to renew it anyway.

Clearly, if the installation was not up to standard three years ago and nothing had been done to it since, it was still not going to be up to standard. But rules are rules, so would I have to pay up.

Another couple of hundred euros.

Kerching!

Mr Potential Buyer, meanwhile, was anxious to start scratching about to see what the existing system consisted of, so he would at least know what he was looking at in terms of a replacement. They can be costly things indeed. Mine was around ten thousand euros and that was only for up to three people. He needed to put in one capable of coping with his family of four children, plus visiting friends and relatives.

I hoped it was not going to turn out to be a deal-breaker.

I arranged another time to meet the would-be buyers at the house so we could scrabble about and see what we could find out. I was determined to show willing, to demonstrate that I was not deliberately hiding any nasty surprises, so I got there before them. I went armed with my big brushcutter, Shindaiwa-san (I name most things, remember). He's almost as big as I am and pretty hefty to wield, but he made short work of all the overgrown brambles behind the house where the tank was likely to be, soon exposing the ground underneath.

When the buyers arrived I was scratched, sweaty, but triumphant. I had won the battle of the brambles and we now had a blank canvas to work with. We could at least get to where we needed to be to start our search.

Of course, Sod's Law decreed that it was only after my efforts that Mr and Mrs Potential Buyer mentioned that their eldest son worked as a landscape gardener, so he could have done the brushcutting for me, undoubtedly with far less effort.

Well, at least they couldn't have accused me of being obstructive.

We dug, dug, dug and scrape-scrape-scraped away, with spades, pickaxes and forks, starting in the logical place, right under the window of a loo. That way, we figured, we would find a waste pipe and could then follow that in search of a tank of some sort.

The trouble was, we were working on the slope at the back of the house. Because it was on a slope, rainfall over the years had washed soil down from the garden at the top and redistributed it lower down. The result was that it was now anyone's guess where the tank might be, and it could be under a foot or two, perhaps more, of now compacted earth.

We decided to give up for the time being. Mr Potential Buyer had a better solution. He knew a man with a mini digger who could come and do the donkey work for us. They were anxious to get him in anyway to give them an estimate for the work necessary to put in the swimming pool they wanted. That would also require a new entrance being created. Good job they were best mates with the mayor, as that certainly couldn't be done without his consent.

In the meantime, I had another expensive inspection to arrange. Any house being sold here needs a *'diagnostique'*, a full health report of anything and everything. It covers such things as identifying any asbestos present, any destructive insects like termites – fortunately absent in this area – and classifying it for energy consumption and the like. Such surveys normally take a couple of hours and cost around three to four hundred euros.

By now you should know that if there's a short straw to be drawn, I will draw it, at least as far as my brother's affairs were concerned. I certainly did with the man who came to do the house inspection. It was nice that he was thorough. It meant no nasty surprises were going to pop up at a later date which could have the buyers coming back on me for failing to disclose things. But he was so slow that, having spent nearly five hours on it, he announced that he had still not finished and needed at least another half day to complete it.

The trouble was, I'd left the dogs at the kennels for the day to free myself up to be there and the rules there are strict. If you don't turn up to collect them at the appointed hour, you have to leave them for the night and go back the next day, and I didn't want to run that risk.

We arranged another appointment for a later date, and I again booked the dogs in to kennels for the day – yet more expense. But this time I warned the man that he had a deadline to meet. He must complete his survey to allow me to leave by four o'clock in the afternoon to go and collect my girls.

The buyers had also arranged for an electrician to come and give them a detailed report on what needed doing to make the power supply safe and get the electrical circuits functioning once more. That was to be on the same day as the *diagnostique* man, who would hopefully take me at my word and finish his task in the time I had appointed for him.

He finally got it done and produced his detailed report. The mini digger man had been but had found nothing of any help to us on the sewage front. Mr Potential Buyer had got two quotes to replace the septic tank, both around the ten thousand Euro mark. He then asked if I could drop the selling price of the house to reflect what he was going to have to pay. I told him I'd think about it.

On the one hand, the price was about as low as I could go and it was not my legal responsibility to fund the new septic tank, or even to make a contribution towards it. On the other hand, I didn't want to risk the buyers pulling out now, with no Plan B in place. I always like to have a Plan B, at least, with everything. I decided to leave him to sweat for a few days.

I was a bit miffed, knowing their plans included installing a swimming pool, which was non-essential, instead of spending the money on a septic tank, which was essential. Especially as they were allowed a full year from the date of purchase to get the work done. I consulted the oracle which is Facebook, to see what my friends and followers thought. The opinion was unanimous. Stick to your guns, Steady the Buffs, and don't drop the price.

In the end, Mrs Potential Buyer cracked before I did, emailing me to see if I had reached a decision. I had. The price remained as we had agreed. Take it or leave it.

She said she'd told her Other Half that would be the answer, although he'd pushed for trying it on. They would, she said, take it. We were all systems go for the sale to go through.

Chapter Eighteen
Meanwhile, on Planet Earth

For the moment, my own life seemed to be stuck on hold. Most of my time and a large part of my thoughts were centred round the whole business of my brother's financial affairs and how to sort them out. Despite three costly lawyers, I felt, a lot of the time, as if I was on my own, paddling my own canoe through shark-infested waters, with no idea where I was heading.

I was still making the journey to the HHofH two or three times a week most weeks to bring stuff back. Then on the intervening days, I would unload and store what I'd brought. Then I'd go through all the paperwork I had collected to see if there were any clues as to where my brother might have had assets and, more worryingly, to start to get a more detailed idea of what liabilities there were. At least the long hot summer meant I could do this work outside in the sunshine. Much more pleasant.

French law is complicated in all cases. Ask any French person and they will tell you as much. This was all going to be much more difficult than normal, with different countries involved. Because there were now buyers waiting to go ahead, Mr France and Mr England had decided between them that the best course of action would be to separate out the French assets from the British ones so the house sale could go through speedily, which is what I wanted.

This involved getting Mr Wales to draw up some sort of

deed to allow that to happen. It was unusual, possibly even slightly unorthodox. Nothing about Mr Wales filled me with any confidence, even less when he asked me what to put in said document. As if I was likely to have any more of a clue than he had.

I was so desperate to have the house, at least, off my hands before winter set in that I would have cheerfully signed anything and possibly donated a kidney to swing the deal. As a result, I didn't quite appreciate the enormity of what I was letting myself in for.

It seems that in splitting the assets up according to country, instead of the outstanding bills being settled by the French estate, then any crumbs left over coming to me, I was going to have to pay them all, in full, up front. That was in addition to having to give the French taxman a chunk of money which was very nearly three times what I'd paid for my grottage. It was either that or run up huge interest rates by way of penalty for late payment. Thank goodness I'd always been thrifty and kept a rainy day fund, sitting quietly in a bank account somewhere. It was about to start pouring down. In fact, it looked as if I was heading for the monsoon season.

At least I'd had one big weight lifted from my shoulders with the prospect of the house sale going ahead. But there were still plenty of other burdens. In France, there is no cause of death given on a death certificate. That presented some problems and some explanations when sending it to various people in the UK who needed a copy.

My brother had taken out life insurance on his bank loan when he bought the Pink House. It's compulsory, in order to cover the loan in the event of the death of the borrower. For the insurers to pay out, they needed a detailed report from his doctor. Rather than just send him the form, or try to explain over the phone what was needed, I decided to go to the medical centre myself to see his doctor in person on my next trip to the HHofH.

My brother's doctor had also been mine, for a time, although I'd tended to see more of one of the other partners in the practice. Just as I was going into the medical centre, clutching the form in my hand, the doctor himself came out of his office, showing out his previous patient. It's not like in many UK practices, where patients are summoned by a digital display screen, or perhaps by the receptionist telling them when it was their turn. Here the doctors usually come out themselves to find their next client, and then they see them out afterwards, with the customary hand-shaking before and after the appointment.

The doctor saw me, recognised me, came straight over, shook my hand and offered his condolences. I explained about the form, he took me into his room immediately and invited me to sit down while I handed it over for him to sign.

Insurance companies, naturally enough, like to find reasons not to pay out, particularly on life insurance. Some won't pay out at all on suicide, others only after a decent interval between when the policy is issued and the death occurs. The ones covering my brother had stringent clauses to do with lifestyle; anything which might precipitate early death had to be declared.

I didn't actually know myself what had caused his death. I knew he hadn't been well, not for a long time. But he'd just spent a few days in hospital on a cardiac ward and it seemed as if this time he hadn't escaped out of the window, so someone must have been happy to let him go. He had been due to go back, probably for some abdominal surgery, but had died before then.

The doctor carefully scrutinised the form and all of its probing questions while I waited with bated breath. He then said he was happy to sign everything and that, in his opinion, the cause of death was a myocardial infarction, a heart attack. He'd been the doctor who had been called to the house when my brother had been found, to certify the death.

It was a relief, in a way, to know that, as it would in all probability have been quick. And on a purely material level it was an even bigger relief to know that the insurance would now pay out the outstanding amount on the mortgage on the house.

In the midst of everything that was going on, I was in desperate need of some normality, some time spent doing the things I enjoyed. I'd had to more or less give up on doing any gardening, which I usually enjoy. There simply wasn't the time to do much with it, even less to do anything with my plot over the road, which was meant to be my kitchen garden. I was always too tired to keep that up, apart from seeding some Swiss chard. As well as being very tasty, it's such an easy, obliging plant, and so cheery, with its bright scarlet colouring.

What I needed most was something to occupy my mind, to stop it from going over worst case scenarios of ending up bankrupt and losing my own home in trying to pay all the bills. Not as far-fetched an idea as it may sound, with the way the bills for the lawyers, the taxman and the various creditors were starting to pile up.

Giving Domi her English lessons was always great fun. We laughed a lot in between the serious study. We had great hilarity over the word lawyer. Traditionally, in France, English has been taught with great emphasis on grammar and the written word, rather than conversational practice. The consequence is that many French people can read and write English reasonably well, but lack the skills and confidence to even attempt pronunciation, except at a basic level.

'Lawyer' was a word Domi had some difficulty in pronouncing, often getting it confused. When she told me one day she had to go and see her 'liar' I couldn't help but laugh. I hastily assured her that it was not at her or her pronunciation but rather that her error was both apt and amusing. And before any lawyers reading this take offence, I'll just throw in that my cousin was a solicitor and his father, my uncle, was a Crown

Court judge. I'm not saying all lawyers are economical with the truth. Just that it has been known to happen.

Salvation in the shape of mental distraction when I was alone was mercifully on hand. To my own surprise, as much as that of people who had been reading the Sell the Pig series, at the end of 2014, I'd started to write crime fiction. It had always been my preferred genre, both to read, having grown up on a diet of Agatha Christie, and to watch on television. But after I'd had a dream which gave me an initial idea, I'd published three crime novels in 2015, one already in 2016, and I was part-way through another when I received news of my brother's death.

Luckily, my main character, Detective Inspector Ted Darling, isn't your typical copper. Not a hard-drinking, smoking, swearing, womanising maverick. Just rather a nice, quietly-spoken bloke with a steady relationship and a load of cats. The sort of person anyone might enjoy spending some time with, especially when feeling down.

Actually, I really can't claim any credit for creating him as he arrived in my head as a perfectly formed character, complete with name, description and all his characteristics and attributes. He's steadfastly refused to leave me in peace ever since. Fortunately, as it happens, as he's become something of a success, with his own fan club.

And I've been very glad of his company for all the driving. As well as chats with my brother, my journey time would be taken up working out new scenes, turning them round in my brain until they felt right. Then I'd eagerly rush home to get them down on the computer while they were still in my memory. I can seldom remember what day it is, but I can still hold my writings in my head.

Because my mother had vascular dementia, as did her elder sister, I've always worried that I will go down the same route. I do plenty of strange, absent-minded things now but, in my mid-sixties and living alone, that's not all that unusual. I often wonder if I would actually be aware if I started to lose the plot. I have taken the precaution of chalking the word 'DOGS' in block capitals on my little blackboard in the kitchen. Not that I think I'll forget that I have some. No chance of them letting me do that. It's just that I feed them twice a day, raw meat for breakfast, then some rice and their fresh fruit and veg smoothie – or smoozees, as the French call them - later in the day and it's that second one I sometimes forget about.

I've always loved writing, ever since I was a small child, and I'm hoping that writing the Ted series will help keep my brain functioning to a degree for a bit longer. I've now brought out six books in the series in two years and Book Seven is already insinuating itself into my brain during my driving time. The miles pass by much more pleasantly in Ted's easy company than alone.

Chapter Nineteen
Scribbling

One of the reasons I was drawn to my little grottage when I first saw it was that I felt it was potentially ideal for me as I got even older. I would have loved the solitude of a detached, isolated property, but it was clearly not practical, buying for the future. I've been lucky with my neighbour in this back-to-back semi. Neighbours can make or break buying a house. Mine is kind and supportive in many ways but not at all intrusive.

At first I wasn't at all keen on the idea of being close to a road. The house is set back a bit, and it's a quiet lane with not a lot of traffic. But it does mean there are passers-by that I can always flag down in times of need, though not all that frequently. And given my propensity for accidents and injuring myself, it's a reassuring thing.

The property was not overlooked, when I first bought it, which was another attraction. There is a small bungalow up the track opposite, but our houses are shielded from one another's sight. It was for sale for some time but currently has a young couple and their small daughter lodging there as tenants. I see the little girl going off to school on the minibus each day and being dropped off again in the afternoon. They start school young here, and the school days are long.

Being on a school bus route is a big advantage. It means the snowplough/gritter does a run here at least once a day in bad weather, so the children can get safely to and from school on the bus.

Having children about means that this sleepy corner of France is starting to be pulled into the twenty-first century with strange, modern customs. I heard my neighbour calling me one evening in October. It was not late but it was already dark. So imagine my surprise to find a scary small witch standing in my driveway, in the company of a taller person wearing a ghoulish mask. The young girl from up the hill, out trick or treating round the tiny hamlet with her sporting father.

I wasn't equipped for dealing with American traditions like that out here in the French sticks. I had no sweets or chocolate of any sort in the house, as I'm trying to cut down on nibbling and snacking. Nor did I have much loose change. I had to scrabble round in the drinks holder in the front of my van in which I keep an emergency supply of coins for the rare occasions I use the motorway and need money for the toll. I'll have to try to remember for next year and be better prepared, although it's not a tradition I have much time for.

Scrabbling was one thing, but my neighbour and I were in for a lot of trouble from scribbling spoiling our quiet and peaceful lives. Or *Gribouille*, to be precise. *Gribouille* is the French word for a short-sighted idiot, but the verb *gribouiller* is to scribble. And the Scribble in question was a dog.

Since I'd bought my grottage, planning permission had been granted to build a large house opposite mine, one which did look down on my property. I'd planted plenty of trees and shrubs to mask it from view, and it was a long time in the building so it had stood empty for a while. But then the young couple moved in and shortly afterwards, they got themselves a dog. Scribble.

It was a border collie. A female. It came sniffing round the front of my property and that of my neighbour one day, but seemed amiable enough and went trotting back home when we shooed it away. The neighbour's little Jack Russell, Étoile, and my Fleur are both a bit gobby with other dogs and Rosie will do whatever big sister Fleur does. So we thought it best not to encourage Scribble to linger, or to want to make frequent visits.

One evening, Domi and I were in my house working away on the complexities of the English language. We heard a noise which sounded rather like Fleur massacring one of her squeaky toys, except that, for once, she was sitting quietly under the table where we were working.

I say we heard it. Domi certainly did. I just heard a bit of a squeak. My hearing is not brilliant, it has to be said. Got to love genetics. My mother, her own mother, and all of her siblings, five in total, had all gone deaf as they got older and all needed hearing aids. My brother and I had also inherited our maternal grandmother's poor eyesight, although his was far worse than mine.

Hindsight is a wonderful thing, and my vision for it is clearly better that my actual vision. I only realised, when I was the last one left on that side of the family, that amongst the many old family photographs, there were hardly any of my mother's mother. In the couple I did find, she was wearing the thick bottle-bottom glasses I remember so well. She clearly didn't enjoy having her photo taken, perhaps because of them, and probably felt vulnerable removing them if she couldn't see a thing when she did.

The state of my hearing came to light more than twenty years ago, when I was living in Dorset. As I was walking through a shopping centre, someone came out of an optician's I was passing and asked if I wanted a free hearing test. I wasn't pressed for time so I agreed, convinced I would waltz through it. I had to listen for sounds and press a button when I heard them. I was surprised and disappointed to be told back then, more than twenty-five years ago, that the hearing in my right ear was below normal. I'd always thought my habit of using the phone to my left ear was just a throwback to my early days as a journalist, taking down shorthand over the phone.

Back then in the seventies, there was no email, no mobile

phones. If a story came in that had to be dictated over the phone, it was always me who got picked to take it down in shorthand as I had the fastest speeds in the office at the time. It was always a case of phone clamped to left ear and right hand scribbling away dementedly with the Teeline shorthand which was taught to journalists as it was quicker to learn than the traditional Pitman.

So with slightly impaired hearing, it's not surprising that I didn't hear as much as Domi and didn't identify the sound for what it really was. It was only when I saw my neighbour the following day that she told me what had happened. As she'd been getting out of her car, just outside her own front gate, and had put Étoile down on the grass ready to go into the garden, disaster had struck, in the form of Scribble. The sheepdog appeared from nowhere - as my neighbour said, like an arrow out of the blue - sank its teeth into the little terrier's leg and refused to let go. The squeaks which we'd heard were, in fact, cries of pain. My neighbour had only managed to rescue her dog by several judicious swings of her handbag to break things up.

Things got worse. Étoile was treated for the initial bite wound, but the injury didn't improve. Instead she seemed to be getting progressively more lame. Further investigation showed that the bite had damaged a ligament which had given way and would require costly surgery to put right.

I know, from personal experience of being head-butted by a horse, which is not to be recommended, that ligaments are the slowest tissues of all to heal, taking far longer than bones and tendons. That was bad enough, but then there was the question of the hefty bill for it all. My neighbour tried presenting it to the dog's owners and got short shrift. They pretty much denied that their dog would do such a thing. But if not Scribble, then who?

My dogs never leave the property without me. Even HRH at her grumpiest wouldn't take on a Jack Russell, nor would any of the stray cats hanging around. And I highly doubted that my neighbour would decide to bite her own dog. The whole incident caused a lot of bad feeling, especially as the owners continued to let their dog run about loose, often clearly not knowing where it was or what it was getting up to.

I'd be working away at my desk sometimes, my dogs playing happily in the garden, the back door open so they could come and go as they pleased and I could keep an eye on them. Then suddenly all hell would break loose, with much barking and canine swearing. I'd race outside to find Scribble hurling itself at my gates, and my dogs putting up a vocal rearguard action to repel boarders and defend their own territory..

Sometimes such punch-ups would be followed by a half-hearted whistle from the dog's owners calling her back. To be fair, she did go back when called, though I wasn't sure she would if she had her teeth sunk into another dog when they whistled her.

I tried calling across to the woman owner when I saw her standing there one time, saying she needed to keep her dog on her own property, and got short-shrift in the form of a less than polite response. I saw little point in going across and trying to negotiate, if that was her attitude.

It meant I had to radically rethink how I took my dogs out. I didn't dare step outside the gate with the two of them on leads, in case the thing came after them. I didn't fancy being caught up in a three-way punch-up, with the increased risk of a fall. I was an expert at falling over of my own volition, without any help from a dog fight. As I got older, I was more worried than ever of sustaining a serious injury, especially with the depleted calcium risks of Silly Coeliac.

Now I have to get the van out every time I want to walk my dogs, to avoid confrontation. I drive about half a mile away and walk them from there. It's an inconvenience, of course, but it's the safest option. The situation also means that all the time and effort I put in with Shindaiwa-san the brushcutter, hacking out a footpath right round the perimeter of my land over the road, was a complete waste of time. The land borders Scribble's garden and neither was fenced, so the risk was just too great for me to use it. I'd planned to use it as an exercise trail for me and the dogs in icy or snowy weather as, being all on the level, there was less risk of falling.

One evening, Fleur decided to take matters into her own paws. It was late, by our standards. I've never been much of a night owl. Recently, as tired as I was, ten o'clock seemed like the middle of the night to me. I'd let the dogs out into the garden for a last pee while I saw to things like switching off the computer, stoking up and shutting Leo the Lohberger, the kitchen range, down to his slowest burn for the night.

Out in the garden, all hell broke loose once again in the form of much barking, snarling, and squealing. Damn! It could only mean another visit from Scribble. I rushed outside and sure enough, Scribble had made the grave error of shoving her head right through the bars of the big double metal gates to my garden, whereupon Fleur had promptly sunk her fangs into Scribble's nose and was hanging on for all she was worth.

Fleur may well be a little thug, but she is a well-trained little thug. She let go as soon as I ordered her to and, with a yelp of relief, Scribble raced off over the road and sprinted up the hill to the safety of her own garden, no doubt sporting some interesting new body piercings.

The situation is far from resolved but at least Scribble, of her own free will, is now showing herself less willing to come down here pestering my two. She does occasionally appear and still goes on a rampage around the hamlet, turning up one time in the bedroom of the people who live down the hill, who were less than amused. Perhaps they should have tried biting her on the nose.

Chapter Twenty
Al-Cat-Traz

I spend a lot of time on social media, it has to be said. Once I got over my initial reticence, I really started to enjoy it. It's a great way to meet and to interact with interesting new people in many different parts of the world. I've always loved strong debates, and there are plenty of those going on any time you open your account.

Sometimes it can get petty, like the school playground, with a lot of name-calling and general nastiness. Some groups have Moderators – I'm one myself in a few – who, like the school prefects, try to make sure that everyone stays civil and behaves themselves. Some people tend to abuse social media, losing no opportunity to plug themselves and whatever it is they're selling. Self-promotion is banned in the Book Group I run but it's amazing how many people ignore the rule. You'd think that anyone being interested in books would at least be able to read the rules.

Social media is a great way to, as the Americans say, 'reach out' to the readers of my various books. I always include my Facebook and Twitter contact details, and an email address, in the books, so people can get in touch. It's lovely how many do and what kind and positive feedback I get for what I write, from all sorts of people.

It does mean that people who follow me, particularly on Facebook, which I find is more personal than Twitter, know me rather too well. So the day I mentioned that I was about to embark on one of my famous Tottie B-I-Y projects (Bodge-It-Yourself) which involved me, up stepladders, over a drop, with power tools, there was a general chorus of warning.

I've always kept the cats shut in the barn on hunting days, for their own safety. But I knew it was neither popular with them, nor all that fair to them. Even in winter, we often get lovely sunny days when Bibi and HRH would be far happier skipping about in the fields massacring the field mouse population than shut in a gloomy barn, even though it is big and has lots of toys for them.

The barn has a hayloft and I'd got Patrick the handyman to build a small deck in front of the door to it, raised a couple of metres off the ground on sturdy big timber posts. I had an idea that if I could somehow make some sort of a cage, a bit like a fruit cage, around it, the cats could at least enjoy lazing around in the sunshine there during days when they were confined to barracks.

I'd made an early prototype using simple meshing, the sort used to keep birds off raspberries and other soft fruit. My initial plan to put a proper flat roof on it had run foul of the concrete screed on the wall. My modest electric drill simply didn't have the guts to make any impression on it, to enable me to fix a batten to which to attach the mesh. As always, I'd had a plan B. I'd crept nervously higher up the ladders than I liked to be and had attached cup hooks to the bottom of the eaves to hang the mesh from there instead.

Bibi thought the entire thing was just about the best game anyone had ever invented for her. She quickly discovered that with some determined head-butting, she could effectively punch a way through the plastic mesh to let herself out. She did it frequently, with much glee. She never went anywhere. She just sat on the outside smiling and purring in satisfaction. I would patiently weave the latest hole back together, then, in the time it had taken me to put the ladders away and the kettle on, she would be there again, outside the cage, all purry smiles and asking when we could play some more. I often wondered if she timed herself, trying to beat her personal best.

Things were about to change, however, with all the equipment I was collecting from the HHofH. For a start, there was a monster of an electric drill, with a bit so long and so substantial it looked as if it could have made the first bore for the Channel Tunnel. That would eat concrete screed for breakfast, even with me operating it.

It's a good job my Facebook friends couldn't have seen me wobbling up the steps with the big beast and trying to hold it still enough to make the first hole without losing control and crashing down onto the deck. I soon had a row of holes, more or less where I'd intended to make them, and none of them in any part of my anatomy, which is no mean feat for me.

I'd recovered enough timber from the HHofH to cover most of my garden in a roof, had I wanted to. Now I had a sturdy cross-member against the wall, it was going to be relatively easy to make sections to form a roof which should hopefully deter even the fiendish Bibi. HRH was easy. She avoided any manual work of any description. I could probably have put up a picture of a roof and it would have been enough to deter her from trying to escape.

My brother clearly had grandiose plans to extend the pens in the garden to contain his growing collection of feral cats, which was good news for me. There was a huge, heavy roll of good quality galvanised chicken netting lying in the long grass of the garden. That was a real blessing as for some reason, it's expensive to buy here. Then there was the world supply of good solid screws and rawl plugs, ideal for the batten to which I intended to attach the roof sections.

For once, I was trying to be sensible and realistic in my plans, keeping the roof sections small enough so I could manoeuvre them into place whilst teetering about on the step ladders, without risking serious injury. I even managed to remember to leave a small gap to put my head and shoulders through to fix panels securely in place from above, then close the space with one section which secured from underneath. When I'd finished, I stood back with some degree of pride to admire my handiwork.

Would you like to hazard a guess how long it took Bibi to find and exploit the first weakness in the structure?

No, it was actually faster than that.

The flaw in my plan, which I should have seen for myself, was that, although I wanted Al-Cat-Traz, as I'd named my construction, to be totally cat-proof on hunting days, there did need to be some sort of trap-door which could be opened and closed on days when the cats were at liberty to come and go as they pleased.

And therein lay the problem. If I could open it to release them, it was only a matter of time before Bibi would learn the trick, too, and I would be back to square one.

Our peaceful life was changing somewhat, and not in a good way. Not only were my dogs under siege from Scribble but poor HRH was in terror for her life, thanks to the thug of a white cat from next door. Neige is the daughter of the local old bruiser of a tom cat, Feu Vert, so called for his green eyes, like traffic lights. He made the mistake of tangling with my dogs one dark night and I never saw him again. His daughter inherited his bad temper and pugilistic genes.

Like all true bullies, she quickly discovered that, despite her haughty demeanour, HRH is a timid little cat who hates confrontation and is very easily picked on. Once the darker evenings arrive, my neighbour doesn't let Neige out as she herself is at work all day so wants to make sure her cat is safely indoors before darkness. Like many white cats, Neige is deaf. She's also arrogant, so when she chooses to cross the road, not only does she not hear oncoming traffic, if she spots it, she clearly expects it to give way to her.

But the summer days can herald a living nightmare for poor

HRH. Sometimes when I'm working at home I hear such a swear-up going on outside and have to rush out to where a poor, small, dark chocolate point part-Siamese princess is getting the stuffing knocked out of her right royally by the much bigger horrible white monster.

Al-Cat-Traz also needed to be sufficiently impregnable to stop Neige getting in, as she thought nothing of sauntering into the barn to bash up HRH. It would be nice to be able to offer her a bit of security in the good weather, without her running the risk of getting attacked.

2016 was also the year we acquired another cat. Not intentionally, of that I can assure you. I noticed that Bibi and HRH seemed to be eating far more than usual, but I put it down to the colder weather coming, reducing prey and increasing their appetites.

During the warm weather, they'd both taken to staying out all night, even HRH. I'd see both of them, lurking about not far away. HRH's favourite place is a large stone slab which covers a spring in the next field. It collects the warmth of the sun during the day, making a nice warm throne for HRH in the evening. It's also an ideal place to hunt lizards which go there to sun themselves.

The girls were back in at a good time most evenings, now that the days were getting shorter, and they seemed to be eating like a pack of wolves, judging by the amount of food they were getting through. One evening as I was filling up feed bowls of crunchies and meaty chunks in sauce, as they'd been once more emptied and licked clean, I heard a hissing sound coming from under a nearby chair. I looked down to see a ginger and white feline face looking at me and spitting in contempt at the choice of food I had put out.

The size of its belly and the way it ate had me worried for a few days that it might be a pregnant female. Then I got a good rear view one day and saw that it was definitely a well-endowed young male. That was one consolation.

Bibi and HRH were not at all thrilled at having a new roomy. I firmly but gently evicted him and shut the trap in Al-Cat-Traz. Back he came. I know not how. We did this a few times. It must have meant that he had found a way in to the barn which even my two had not yet discovered as a means of escape. And if anyone can find an escape route, it's usually Bibi.

He was a pleasantly smiling cat, but I didn't want to keep him. Two is enough for me. The current half-time score at this point was Ginger-job 10, Tottie 0.

Apart from wherever the interloper was getting in, Al-Cat-Traz was getting closer to being as secure as I would like it. My mission was finally to make it impregnable. I had already vanquished HRH but not yet Bibi who is part cat, part ferret. She seems to have the ability to turn herself into liquid, like mercury, and pour herself through the smallest gap I've overlooked.

I still spend a lot of time touching up my efforts. I am determined to win. Unfortunately, Bibi is equally as determined that she will emerge the victor. As I work, she sits in a flowerpot, getting stoned on cat nip and smiling inscrutably at me.

Chapter Twenty-one
Train-train

The French have a wonderful expression for humdrum daily routine. *Train-train*. I love it. It so perfectly describes how life goes trundling on and on, like a model train. Round and round on the same tracks, stopping at the same places on its way.

My life is a bit like that. It would doubtless bore the pants off most people, but it suits me ideally. I have my *petit train-train*, my little template for the day. It helps me to avoid forgetting anything important. I admit it does, at times, border on the obsessive.

I like the same brand of tea at certain times of day. Earl Grey for the mornings, Lady Grey for the afternoons. Never the other way round. I love my big bowl of frothy coffee with cinnamon sprinkles for elevenses and have been known to get grumpy if I miss it for any reason.

I watch Coronation Street on television. Goodness knows why, as it's going steadily downhill of late. But it's a hard habit to break. I like watching crime drama and true crime, then dissecting the latest offering with friends on social media. I love watching Holby City, too. Fleur likes the theme music to that, the boo-boom of the heartbeat which proceeds the music.

I like going to the library and the local market in Olliergues on Saturdays. This has become such a habit that if I have to go to Olliergues on any other day for some reason, the day automatically becomes a Saturday in my head and completely confuses me, until I get back in sync.

I've now been in my little grottage for five years and I slowly seem to have been accepted by most of the people around. Instead of the wary chin-lift of greeting, some of them are now giving me a nod and even, occasionally, a mouthed *'bonjour'* as I drive past in my brightly coloured and unmistakable hippymobile with the stickers all over it. As well as the poppies, the dragon and the other images, there are sayings like 'Where have all the hippies gone?' and 'Give peace a chance', which intrigue my French neighbours as I drive past.

I even seem to have won the approval of the stern lady in the post office, which is no mean feat. She has a disapproving look, when it suits her, and never takes the trouble to hide it. It's always obvious who doesn't reach her high standards. But latterly, I am greeted with smiles and even the occasional exchange of pleasantries about the weather, a high accolade indeed.

It's never been my intention to make waves in my new community nor to Anglicise any aspect of it. I love it just as it is. But, inadvertently, I have introduced a little touch of England in the form of a victory in the War of the Roses.

It's long been hotly contested which country produces the best roses, England or France. It's almost as contentious as the British War of the Roses, between the houses of Lancaster and York. I should, as I type this, be waving the red rose of Lancaster, in honour of my Lancastrian ancestors. But I have to confess I'm not a fan of red roses. I prefer white and pink ones.

I grow quite a few roses. I love plants which are strongly perfumed, like roses and lilies. I won't give soil space to anything without a scent, unless it has some other outstanding quality, such as being vital to pollinators or birds.

When an old friend died and left me a few pounds, I bought myself ten roses from David Austin, the famous British rose growers. All are gold medal winners for their fragrance and they really are stunning, both to look at and to enjoy the perfume, especially on a warm summer evening.

My neighbour and I often chat over the fence and share the odd thing. She gives me chives she grows in pots in her garden. I sometimes give her some cake as I know she also tries to eat gluten free, which she finds helps with her ailments.

One day we got talking roses. I'd just come back from yet another trip to the HHofH. There's a rather pretty apricot tea rose which grows on the patio there, but for me its beauty is diminished by the fact that it has no scent at all. I mentioned my medal winners and promised to give her a couple of blooms from the best of them all, Gertrude Jekyll, which I duly did.

She was an instant convert. One day I spotted her taking her post in from the letterbox outside her front gate. The French system of postal delivery is brilliant. Every household is required to have a post box at the furthest extremity of the property, and they are large enough to accommodate moderate-sized parcels. The posties have a master key to open them, so if you're waiting for something important and have to go out, as long as it fits in the box, the postman can leave it for you, safely locked away until your return.

The various parcel couriers are different as not all of them have keys, so they often try to use their initiative, with varying degrees of success. One bright spark decided to leave me a parcel, in a brown cardboard box, inside my barn, when I was out. Fair enough. Only he left it amongst the pile of brown cardboard boxes stacked ready for burning, so it was a couple of days before I found it.

The bag my neighbour was carrying to the house from her post box was unmistakably from David Austin. When she saw me looking, she admitted she had been so captivated by the fragrance of my rose that she had ordered one herself.

The British, eh? Conquering France, one rose at a time.

I'd also made some headway in being seemingly accepted, to a degree, by my neighbour's elderly father. He was always perfectly polite whenever he saw me, always the customary *'bonjour, madame'*, but that was about it.

I was therefore surprised when, one day, he rang the bell on my gate and stood there with a generous box of windfall apples from his orchard over the road, which adjoins my plot of land. All that separates the two is a post and plain wire fence, two strands high.

At some point the wire had come down in a couple of places. I think the neighbouring farmer's tractor, when it was mowing grass around the trees, had got a bit too close and broken it. I do know that in my enthusiastic wielding of Shindaiwa-san the brushcutter on my side, I'd managed to catch the wire around the wildly spinning head a couple of times and mangled it some more.

Because I have farming genes, I've managed a couple of equestrian centres, and owned a smallholding, I don't like broken fences, even where there is no livestock involved. One day when I had a bit of time, and some energy, I went over there to repair it. And not a Welsh farmer type repair, either, with bits of baler twine. I did a proper job, with lengths of the right type of wire, correctly spliced into the gaps and the tension taken up so it was just right. If I say so myself, it was a thoroughly presentable piece of fencing when I'd finished with it.

It clearly surprised and impressed the neighbour's father so much that he brought the apples as a reward, with his effusive thanks. He was no doubt amazed that *'l'Anglaise'* could do such things. It's a habit of country folk in many areas to assume that anyone moving into their midst automatically has to be a townie.

Another good thing about my next-door neighbour is she knows everyone. She's the ideal go-to person when you're looking for someone to do something specific for you. Like a human Google. I just go to our dividing fence, enter the search term, for example, 'do you know anyone who can transport some metal sheets for me?' and, as fast as any search engine, I have the results I need.

The metal sheets were an interesting episode. I was making strides in gradually clearing out the HHofH, although it was painfully slow progress. I was trying to cherry pick anything which I could sell for a few bob as the bills were piling up and I sometimes felt I was drowning in them.

I so nearly missed something which might have been worth a bit, until my brother's friend Neil asked me in an email one time if I'd found the copper sheets. Copper sheets? Of course! I remembered that my brother had mentioned buying a load of thin copper sheets as part of some solar power project or another he was going to embark on, one day. I'd forgotten all about them and I knew the price of copper was high, on a par with that of gold.

The next time I went to the HHofH I had a good rummage round and found them, stashed behind the door in the darkness of the laundry room beyond the garage. I could so easily have overlooked them and they were potential treasure trove.

They were thin and bendy, two metres long by a metre wide. Slightly longer than the back of my van but, I figured, if I could load them standing on their long side and slide them up alongside the front passenger seat, that might just work, although it would rather restrict my vision on that side.

I didn't think they would be all that heavy, but because they were thin sheet metal, I took the precaution of putting on thick leather gardening gloves, not relishing the thought of slicing off a fingertip or two.

Picture, if you will, the sight of little old me, trying to wrestle with something like a giant musical wobble board, as made famous by a now-disgraced Australian singer, but with knife-sharp edges and a total will of its own. The more I fought with it, the more it seemed hell-bent on trying to decapitate me or at least to amputate one of my extremities.

In the end, discretion being the better part of valour, and all that, I returned home without the murderous metal and instead asked my neighbour if she knew of a Man with Van who could help me to tame and transport them.

Within an hour, her brother-in-law had phoned to offer his services and those of his 4x4 to go and pick up the copper and anything else which I couldn't manage on my own, all for the price of his diesel.

In between my adventures, while I catch my breath for the next round, my own life follows its peaceful, hum-drum *train-train*. I did somehow find the time to step outside my comfort zone and do an Open University Forensic Psychology module in witness interview techniques, to help Ted with his work. It was fascinating. I've no idea how I managed it. Some day I'll do some more modules and pass the knowledge on to Ted.

I have become so boringly predictable that as soon as I walk into the local cheese shop, the lady is already picking up the Cantal Entre Deux, my favourite, to which I am seldom unfaithful. But as I told her, when something is that good, why change? I do occasionally go mad, on high days and holidays, and get some of the *chevre enrobé*, goat's cheese rolled in dried fruit. It comes in various varieties, of which my favourite is cranberry and kumquat.

I did surprise her the other day by treating myself to some of the more expensive Salers cheese, too. My friend Jill told me she'd recently heard on no less an authority than the BBC that it's unique as it's the only cheese known to be capable of destroying the listeria bacterium.

Sounds like a good enough excuse for eating it to me.

Chapter Twenty-two
The birds fly again

People seem to be surprised that two of my best friends are both called Jill. I'm not sure if the surprise is at the names being the same or that fact that I have two friends. Actually, I don't like to confuse the issue but I actually have three friends called Jill.

I'm not a person who has a massive circle of people I call true friends, but it does so happen that two of my besties are called Jill. To keep it simple here, I shall refer to them as Jill, my oldest and dearest friend, from Wales, and Jilli, alias Doris, a newer but still close friend, originally from Yorkshire, but now living in Italy.

Jill from Wales had helped me make a huge difference to the HHofH. But there was still an overwhelming amount to do and time was starting to become pressing, now there were buyers on the scene. There was also the prospect of a quick sale, once they'd sorted their finances out. It was time for reinforcements.

Doris, in Italy, had offered to come and lend a hand, once her busy summer season was over. Doris is a real grafter, no stranger to work, and always full of ideas. She'd recently converted a former goat shed on her property into a beautiful, cosy cabin for 'glamping' – glamorous camping – and had been doing a roaring trade with visitors wanting to discover her part of Italy, with its walking and wildlife.

Doris, some of you will remember, is one of the infamous 'Three Birds' with whom I'd jointly written a travel memoir, Take Three Birds. She'd been here once before, when we were writing the book together, and she and her co-driver had succeeded in turning a straightforward eight-hour journey into a protracted twelve-hour one.

Now she was kindly proposing to make the journey on her own, just to spend a few days giving me a hand. It was a truly generous offer, which I was more than happy to take up. A bit of company, especially from someone who was not afraid of hard work, was just the tonic I needed to help me forge ahead. My only reservation was how spectacularly lost would she manage to get this time, and was a journey like that really sensible to make alone?

She announced that she would set off in the wee small hours, stop to rest as and when she needed to, so would be with me by early afternoon. I'd heard that before – the last time! I gave her strict instructions on no account to turn on the abomination that is 'prat-nav' once she got into France, but to follow the instructions I carefully wrote out for her.

I checked and double-checked everything online through Via Michelin – they're a local company, Michelin, so they should know the roads in this *département* – and with my printed road map. I wrote the name of the town she needed to look out for, to take the correct exit from the motorway, in block capitals. NOIRÉTABLE. It was surely burnt into her brain after missing it last time. She wouldn't make the same mistake twice.

Who am I kidding? This is Doris we're talking about!

I got a few text updates on the journey. Always reassuring to know about someone else's toileting habits, but whatever, I got to share every pee stop. Then I got a triumphant text saying she'd be with me in half an hour.

Déja-vu? Heard that one before, too.

It was turning into a very long half hour, even by Doris's

standards. Then I got a phone call. An actual phone call. And our Doris is someone who doesn't do phone calls. Last time, she had Farmer Bird in the passenger seat to do the talking for her. This time, of course, travelling alone, she had to do the actual vocal stuff.

She was lost, she told me.

Where? I asked.

No idea. She'd run out of motorway and now didn't know which way to head for.

Now I was puzzled because there was no way she should have run out of motorway if she'd followed the instructions.

What about Noirétable? Had she been through there?

I'm not sure which of us was feeling the more frustrated. She can't have been more than an hour away at most, was tired and no doubt getting fed up of driving, but without knowing where she was, I couldn't begin to direct her to where I was. At least, this time, she wasn't staring at the statue of Vercingétorix in the centre of Clermont-Ferrand, as last time. That was something.

I asked what road signs she could see and was able to discount several destinations as being in entirely the wrong direction. In the end I opted for telling her to head for Thiers then call again for more directions.

I was, as usual, out in my garden to take the phone call, the signal always being so poor inside my house. It just happened that my neighbour was also in hers at the same time. I'd told her I had the same mad friend as last time once again driving over from Italy so she was amused to hear that the same thing had gone wrong this time as last.

Time was passing and there were no further calls or texts. I'd planned to suggest, on the next phone call, that if I could get her somewhere close to, I'd go out in the van to pilot her in.

Then, just as I was really starting to get anxious, a wine-coloured Land Rover came trundling up the road. How appropriate, for a wine-drinker like her. And there was Doris, climbing out and laughing at yet another Lost in France adventure.

Once she'd got to Thiers, she explained, she'd remembered the garage where we'd had such drama trying to put LPG in the little Fiat she'd come in last time, and had managed to negotiate her own way from there. She'd decided not to jinx things by stopping to announce that she was finally somewhere she recognised and would be with me soon

I did some checking up afterwards to find out what had gone wrong this time. France has a bizarre habit of changing its road numbers and motorway exit numbers as frequently as some people might change their hair colour. I'd given Doris what I thought was the correct exit number for Noirétable but that section of motorway had been renumbered so she'd sailed on by.

But she was here now, and we had plans for a couple of days' hard graft at the HHofH. First, though, as a bit of a treat for both of us, I was treating her to lunch at my favourite restaurant the following day, to boost our strength and build up morale for what lay ahead. Naturally, it would have to be followed by a visit to the local soap factory. We were both a bit addicted to their products, as is everyone, once they discover them.

I'd told Doris that she was welcome to take anything she spotted at the HHofH which might be of any use to her for her latest project. She'd decided to build a 'hobbit house', undeterred by the fact that she'd neither read the book nor seen the film, so wouldn't know a hobbit if she met one. She's not a fantasy fan. Nor am I, to be strictly accurate, but I do love Tolkien's ability to seamlessly blend light and dark, poetry and prose, tragedy and comedy. I loved the books and I even, in a completely different way, liked the films.

There were still a lot of power tools at the house, including some serious circular saws which looked as if they would come in very handy for building any kind of house, never mind a hobbit house. One expensive piece of kit looked as if it had never been taken out of its box.

We were going to do two trips there. The first, half a day, leaving the dogs at home, we would go in the Land Rover, basically on a recce mission and to stuff in anything we could, things which I couldn't carry myself. Then the next day, the dogs would go off to 'playschool' for the day and we could take both vehicles to bring back twice the cargo.

Doris has a good eye for a nice piece of furniture. She'd studied restoring it at night school. So it didn't take long for her to spot the once expensive and well-made leather three-piece suite in the sitting room. There was a two-seater settee, in not too bad condition, but, like most things in the house, it stank of cat pee. I drew a veil over the big three-seater. I knew its full history and wouldn't inflict it on anyone, nor would it remotely fit in the back of the Land Rover.

Her Land Rover isn't a 'proper' Landy; it's more of a showy thing, with not even as much payload as my Renault Kangoo van. After much measuring and debating, we decided we could just about stuff the smaller sofa in the back of her vehicle. With a lot of grunting and giggling, we loaded it to take to my house on the first trip so it could be thoroughly scrubbed and disinfected for the long trip back to Italy. As it was, we needed the windows open with it on board.

It actually came up so well that I later went back for the armchair. The seat of that was worse, as I'd given Doris the best of the cushions. There's a local upholsterer, though, who can no doubt make me a cushion to match it. It's a nice piece. I'm glad, in the end, I decided to have it, as a memory.

On our second trip, with both vehicles, we took a picnic with us, as we were there for the day. I'd normally have driven us both to a picnic spot nearby to eat our lunch but both vehicles were already partly laden. I had a plan, though. Doris clearly thought I'd lost the plot when I suggested we climb out of the top story window to sit on the roof over the sitting room beneath us. It was a sun-trap on the coolest of days and had a magnificent view across to the Forez mountains, where my grottage is situated.

Loading Doris's vehicle for the return trip after her stay became like the old British TV show, The Generation Game, back in the days of Larry Grayson. Contestants had to watch prizes going past on a conveyor belt in a certain length of time, then anything which they could remember, they won. The prizes were often a bit naff and they always included a cuddly toy.

Various stars presented the show over the years, including Bruce Forsyth, but Larry Grayson always stood out as trying the hardest to help the contestants by suggesting answers to them. People of the right generation will still laugh when someone trots out the old joke, 'Dinner service...fondue set...Cuddly toy! Cuddly toy!'

In this case, the answer to the question, 'How many items can you fit in the back of a Land Rover for a ten-hour road trip' is: Leather sofa. Two metal garden chairs. A mirror. A DVD player. A circular saw. Table linen. Ship's decanter. Bristol blue glass bowl. Camping stove. Cuddly toy!'

Chapter Twenty-three
Peter and the wolf

My brother was always musical. He played the piano well, so our parents bought one for him to practise on at home, and paid for him to have lessons. We both studied music at our separate schools, though he continued to a higher level than I did. He always claimed I was the spoilt one who got everything, but I was never bought a violin. I had to play one borrowed from school.

One piece I remember us both studying and listening to was Prokofiev's Peter and the Wolf. We had a recording of it, 'Appreciating the Orchestra, Part 2'. It was a way of learning the different instruments of the orchestra and what they sounded like. I still remember most of them, and most of the themes of the different characters. The bird was the flute, the cat the clarinet, Peter the string section and the big, bad wolf was the horns.

Because I was young when I first started listening to it, the story became confused in my child's brain with the Aesop fable about the boy who cried wolf; someone who was always making up stories, one of which finally came true. The moral of the fable was 'nobody believes a liar even when they are telling the truth.'

Part of my confusion was due to my mother's dramatic reading aloud skills. She had a great way of making a story sound really scary, just by the emphasis she put on different words. I'm not sure she was always a hundred per cent accurate in how she read things, though, as I have a distinct memory of her reading, 'Just then, a big, grey wolf DID come out of the forest.' And that 'Did' of emphasis doesn't appear in the original, which changes the meaning significantly.

For those who don't know their Prokofiev, the story is about a grandfather warning his grandson, Peter, about being alone in the meadow outside the farm because of wolves in the nearby forest. Peter claims not to be afraid of wolves so his grandfather takes him back to the farm and locks the gate for his own protection. But a duck has followed Peter out and it gets swallowed by the wolf. I was always sorry for the duck.

The Aesop fable is about a shepherd boy who was always shouting out that there was a wolf near the sheep, so people would run to his aid, only to find it wasn't true. So when a wolf did one day appear, his flock was scattered to the four winds as the villagers, fed up of his games, refused to come and help him.

When it came to his health, my brother was a lot like the Aesop fable and the boy who cried wolf. In his case, it was more like, if he claimed to have enough illnesses, on the law of averages, one day, one of them would be genuine. He was fond of quoting Spike Milligan's epitaph, 'I told you I was ill,' which is actually written in Gaelic on Milligan's tombstone: *'Duirt me leat go raibh me breoite.'*

My brother had always been an accomplished hypochondriac, expending a lot of time and energy in looking up symptoms and claiming various obscure illnesses. Some of them were possibly genuine, but he was always rushing round to his doctor and demanding specialist referrals to get them diagnosed. They seldom were. It was more a case of, 'well, it could be that,' which he would always take as solid confirmation that he had whatever the latest self-diagnosis was.

The internet is a very dangerous place for hypochondriacs. In less than half an hour, they can diagnose themselves with several obscure terminal illnesses. It was much harder when it involved going round to the library and looking in real books.

My brother had quite an extensive knowledge of medical matters as he had trained and qualified as a paramedic. This made him even more dangerous. As a ship's purser in the Royal Fleet Auxiliary, he would often double as ship's doctor when the crew complement was too small to warrant a ship's surgeon on board. He had also run his own private ambulance company for a few years when he lived in Wales.

He had become rather more paranoid than ever of late, and his self-diagnoses were getting more inventive. At the risk of sounding as bad as him, I did wonder if he was suffering latterly from Wernicke-Korsakoff syndrome, an alcohol-related type of dementia, one of the symptoms of which can be confabulation, making up stories. He'd always been good at that, but lately they had become rather more extreme.

He had become convinced that his computer was 'possessed' in some way, because it would scroll by itself. I tried the Occam's Razor approach of telling him that when mine started doing that, I'd found it was usually because the mouse was so clogged up with dog hairs it had developed a life of its own. Knowing the number of cats he had, I suspected that his problem was the same.

But no. Nothing quite so mundane for him. His had to be far more dramatic. He sent me an email, entitled, '*Please understand this, I mean it.*'

It read (sic): '*this feckin computer is going to kill me. Whatever I try to do, it fights back, especially when I am on google, whatever I search for, like Meridian Hotel Manchester, it opens the page but then scrolls up and down like someone else is controlling it. I shout and scream at the feckin thing and bang the table but it is going to give me a stroke before long. Perhaps Alex can do something with it if I am still alive in May.*'

Alex, my great friend, is a computer expert, who often

visited around May. It may well have been prophetic on the part of my brother, in a sense. He was prone to uncontrollable rages at the slightest thing. I always tried to bring him back to reality by pointing out the probable cause was almost certainly more innocuous.

It was the same with the illnesses to which he laid claim. One of them involved his conviction that he had the larvae of fruit flies burrowing out of his skin and causing eruptions along his eyebrows. One of the last times I saw him, he was telling me this and kept insisting I 'look, look at that,' jabbing a finger towards his face. The truth was, I couldn't see anything. No signs of lesions and certainly no signs of any larvae erupting anywhere.

It was true that he was plagued with flies in the house but having seen, after his death, the state the place was in, that was hardly surprising. But his suggestion that it could be Myiasis was just laughable. It's a disease of tropical and sub-tropical climates, and even if he had been on tourist trips to India and Africa more than twenty years ago, it was not likely to be that.

For many years, he had believed he was suffering from ME, Myalgic Encephalomyelitis, a notoriously difficult illness to diagnose. That started back in the eighties when we were both living in Wales. I would sometimes drive him to ME Association meetings in Cardiff, so he could benefit from group support.

Afterwards that diagnosis was changed to lupus, but by whom, I'm not sure, as it's another one that's hard to detect. Later still, he managed to get himself referred to St Thomas's Hospital in London to see Professor Hughes, who had given his name to an illness he first discovered, which is also called antiphospholipid syndrome. It's an autoimmune condition which thickens the blood and increases the risk of blood clots and therefore of things like thromboses, heart attacks, strokes and pulmonary embolisms.

A good friend on Facebook reminded me that autoimmune

diseases tend to run in families. They also like to cluster together. Once you have one, you might well start forming a collection, if you're very lucky. And of course, my Silly Coeliac is one of them. She suggested I should get tested for antiphospholid syndrome as it had, after all, been a heart attack which had killed my brother, and he was only sixty-seven.

There's a lot of heart disease on Mother's side of the family and I do have a slight heart murmur. I'd also recently been having problems with dry mouth and eyes – possibly Sjogren's syndrome – and I already have Raynaud's (white fingers and other extremities in the cold) though not badly. So off I trotted to my doctor to ask if, in light of my family history, I should get checked out for Hughes' Syndrome as a precaution.

My doctor is excellent, a good diagnostician, who has young doctors with her on their internship, always an encouraging sign that a doctor knows their stuff. She agreed that blood tests might be a good idea. She also wanted to refer me to a consultant at the big university hospital in Clermont-Ferrand, a regional centre of excellence in internal medicine. She suggested, in addition, a visit to a dermatologist about a persistently itchy patch of skin on my leg which may or may not be eczema, and which was refusing to respond to various standard topical treatments.

I mentioned to her that I'd always suffered from migraines when I was young but had grown out of them after the change. They were sneaking back and they can often be a sign of Hughes' Syndrome, although they can also be triggered by stress and I'd certainly felt plenty of that recently. She instructed the nice young male intern who was with her to carry out a neurological test on me while she started typing out letters of referral to the various specialists. Not all doctors here employ secretaries; sometimes they do everything themselves, which is why consultations can be lengthy.

I felt my face getting a bit hot as he was examining me, but that does happen to me sometimes so I thought nothing of it.

Especially since these days I don't often get to strip off in front of young men. The intern, on the other hand, got very excited, calling my doctor over to see my 'butterfly wing rash' on my face.

Oh, that old thing. It happens to me frequently enough for me to ignore it, but it is distinctive. And it is a characteristic of lupus, as it was thought to resemble a wolf's mask, hence the name. My doctor came over to have a look and the two of them peered and nodded and agreed it looked like a characteristic lupus eruption.

One of the best things about French life, when we first moved here, was the much shorter waiting times for medical appointments than in the UK. All that is changing now. I must wait nearly three months to see the consultant about my various possible autoimmune add-ons. I feel as if my body has become a computer, constantly wanting the latest app to add to its collection.

The wait for a dermatologist is nearer to six months, unless I choose to go and see one in the big city. Considering I turn into a complete bumbling imbecile driving in any town these days, I'll pass on that and continue to wait for the one in nearby Thiers. Mind you, I have managed to get myself quite spectacularly lost in some of its back-streets before now. At least, for the big hospital, I can park the van on the edge of town and go in on the tram.

One thing we are still lucky with here is blood tests. The nurse comes out to your house in rural areas, which is marvellous, especially for fasting tests. Mine was very interested as I was her first ever for an antiphospholipid test – it is quite rare and is under-diagnosed – and it involved quite a lot of phials.

My doctor promised that if anything untoward showed up on the blood test results, she'd call the hospital herself and get me bumped up the list. The initial blood tests for Hughes came back clear, but it is a condition which can give false negatives so it's not yet been ruled out. Ironically, the only result which was outside the norms, being slightly elevated, was for a liver enzyme. And as I've spent more of my life being teetotal than being a drinker, it would be the ultimate cruel twist of fate if there turned out to be anything wrong with my liver.

Chapter Twenty-four
The signing

It's no good. My Word Association (Football) is so over-developed that just the fact of typing that word, signing, has immediately transported my butterfly brain a thousand feet up a Welsh plateau to when I once spent time snowed up alone reading Stephen King's The Shining. Especially as the first real snow of this winter has just started to fall outside.

For me, The Shining is King's best book. It was certainly a menacing one to read all alone cut off from civilisation and with the phone lines down. The film of the book with Jack Nicholson is also pretty powerful stuff, and I also watched that whilst incarcerated alone. This was in the days long before mobile phones or the internet. I thought I was a bit modern having a cordless telephone. With the phone lines down, I genuinely had no contact with the outside world, unless I battled sub-zero temperatures and deep snow drifts to ride down to the village on one of my horses, across the wind-swept moor, as the roads were completely blocked to traffic. Even the snowplough got stuck. I was lucky the power lines held out as long as they did – long enough to watch the film – before they, too succumbed to the weight of ice and snow.

The actual signing in question had nothing to do with thrillers, although it was quite thrilling. We were approaching the stage of being able to sign the *compromis de vente* on the Hammer House of Horrors, the equivalent of exchanging contracts in the UK.

With my French *notaire*, Mr France, being in a different *département* some considerable distance away, it was decided and agreed by all parties that the most practical course of action would be for the signing (Redrum, Redrum! Means nothing if you've not read the book or seen the film but my brain is stuck in that mode now) to take place at the office of the buyers' *notaire*. It was situated in the small town of Combronde, not far from my brother's house.

A date was agreed and I said that for me, because of the journey time involved for me to drive over there, it would need to be late morning or early afternoon. The buyers' *notaire* came back with a time of four o'clock. That wouldn't do at all as it would mean my entire return journey would be made in the dark and these days, I avoid driving in the dark as much as I avoid driving in big towns. I wanted to get the contracts signed as soon as possible, clearly, but not at the expense of a stressful drive home in the dark afterwards.

Signing any document of any description in France is a lengthy process. Every single sheet has to be initialled then at the end it has to be marked as *'lu et approuvé'* (read and approved) then signed with a full signature as well as the date and location where the signature was made.

Cheques here are also signed with the addition of the location where they were signed. Such a simple gesture yet a great help in tackling fraud, surely? If someone presents a cheque supposedly written out by me and with Olliergues as the place of signing and I can prove that on the day in question I was somewhere else entirely, that must surely aid an investigation.

So with all that signing to do, not to mention wading through pages of French legalese, I knew that by the time it had gone on, I would be tired out of all proportion and not fit for anything, certainly not being alert enough to drive home in the dark. My night-time vision has never been brilliant. It's certainly getting worse the older I get.

The buyers were starting to panic, saying if it didn't get signed then it would delay the completion date and blah-blah-blah. I was as keen as they were to get it all done and dusted but there would be little point me signing the draft contract then killing myself in a road accident on the way back. They'd then have to start the process all over again to buy the house from my heirs.

After a frantic exchange of emails between me and Mrs Potential Buyer, it was agreed that they would drive over to Augerolles the morning after they had signed the draft contract at their *notaire*'s. I had a doctor's appointment in the town and we could meet by the church, an easy landmark to find. Although the buyers would have my address on the contracts, it's not easy to find the house and for some reason I was hesitant about the idea of them being able to pitch up on my doorstep at any time unannounced. Then I could sign the documents and they could return them immediately to their *notaire*.

It was a chilly and breezy morning when we met for the signing. I'd gone armed with my current library book, both in case Mr and Mrs Potential Buyer were late and also to pass the time in the doctor's waiting room afterwards. She never ran to time, but given the amount of attention she gave to each patient, me included, I could hardly be critical of that.

In fact the buyers were exactly on time. It looked as if they may actually have arrived before me and gone off for a coffee before we met. That was a good start.

My visit to the doctor was just to check up that there was a good reason why my heart appeared to have joined a country dance group and kept doing a little rendition of the Highland Fling from time to time. I wouldn't normally have bothered, but with the possibility of the risk of a blood-clotting disorder, and with my brother's sudden death, I was taking no chances.

Mrs Buyer was all smiles but, because I'd mentioned I was

currently seeing my doctor and awaiting medical tests and results, she said it had been a good job that I hadn't been at the actual signing the day before because it had almost been a non-event.

The plot where my brother's house had been built at the end of the 1970s had recently been reclassified as agricultural land. Ridiculous, really, as because of the type of land and the size of the plot, it wouldn't be any use for anything other than a couple of sheep, and there are not many of those in the area.

But it did mean that, according to Mrs Buyer, their *notaire* had advised them to think very carefully before signing. Of course, I was only getting all of this second hand so I had no idea as to whether it was accurate or not. But according to what she said, the zoning change meant that, if the house were to burn down, for example, they might not automatically get planning permission to rebuild it. Luckily, the buyers were big buddies of the mayor, a very powerful person in French local politics. They'd phoned him, he'd come straight over and gone through all the documents with them and the *notaire* and declared it safe for them to sign.

I was heartily relieved to hear that, and not to have been present for any of it. I'm not sure my tap-dancing ticker could have taken that amount of excitement.

We stood out in the cold, the documents spread out on the bonnet of my hippymobile, under the watchful eyes of Horus, the Egyptian sky god, and a big red Chinese dragon, just some of my stickers from Hippy Motors UK. I was hoping between them they would keep an eye on things and see that the signing went well and led to an early and successful completion.

Once it was signed, the buyers' *notaire* would send a copy to mine and we would be ready to rock and roll, as soon as their bank loan came through, which they were confident would be soon. Completion could be within a month, two at the most, and that was going to be the most massive weight off my shoulders.

It was not only the financial relief of cashing in a major asset of the estate. It was the prospect of not having to keep doing the drive over there, especially with winter still ahead of us, and not having to pay taxes, insurance and the like to keep a building standing empty. I was trying not to count my chickens too soon, but this was an important first step and the signs were looking good.

Mr Buyer asked if, now we had exchanged contracts, I would let them store a bed, which they were buying for one of their daughters for when they moved into their new home, at the HHofH as they had no room for it at their present home. He also suggested that, if I was willing to entrust him with a key, he could go in occasionally and light the woodburner, to stop the house from getting too cold once the winter weather set in.

I was a bit reluctant. It seemed like a step too far. I reminded them that they did not own the house yet and wouldn't until we had all signed the final contract and they had paid for it. But anything which lessened the frequency of the trips I was having to make seemed like a good idea to me. So I let him have a key to the padlock on the front gate and one for the downstairs apartment, which would give him access to the rest of the house.

He said they would move the bed in there for storage at the weekend, but would always let me know when they were visiting the place and would, of course, let me know if anything appeared to be out of order there.

It was reassuring, in a sense, to have eyes on the ground, keeping a lookout on the house. I had it insured, but it was a relief to know that someone was at least seeing it daily. Mrs Buyer went walking most days with Mrs Mayor, she told me, and their preferred route always took them past the HHofH.

Things were looking promising. Perhaps I could start to relax a bit and encourage my heart to take up a slow and stately waltz rhythm instead of its preferred frenetic foxtrot.

Chapter Twenty-five
Witchy-woo

Lots of people claim to have second sight; the gift, witchy-woo powers, whatever they care to call it. I'm not saying I have. But one thing I do know is that I often know things, before they happen. Not guess or think, but know with a certainty. And the great thing about writing travel memoirs is people can check back on what I said previously, if they don't believe me.

My mother was the same. After I'd left home, when I visited her and we were planning when we'd next see one another, she would often say that it couldn't be on a certain date as something important was happening that day, although she couldn't remember what. On one occasion, the date she mentioned turned out to be the day when her mother-in-law, my Luxembourg granny, died.

I probably inherited it from her because I'm the same. Not always, and I have no control over it, unfortunately. No, I can't predict winning lottery numbers or anything of any material use. But I do sometimes have a total conviction about something which turns out to be true.

Take Brexit, for example. Personally, I'd rather not. It's not that I think that everything about the European Union is marvellous. Far from it. It's just that I believe there needed to be more certainty about the implications of such a momentous decision before it was taken. I felt I didn't know enough about what would happen so I voted to remain. The status quo seemed a slightly safer option than the unknown. I have friends who voted to leave and their reasoning is sound so I respect their choice, even though I don't agree with it.

But you may well remember that some years back, I decided to hedge my bets and apply for French citizenship, because I had one of my strong 'feelings' that Brexit would happen. Well, the term Brexit hadn't been coined back then, but there were early mutterings of a split from Europe and I wanted to be prepared.

I was mocked. People said I was being ridiculous. There would be no such split. There would never even be a vote on it. In the early days, the only talk of it was coming from UKIP, the United Kingdom Independence Party, the Eurosceptic right-wing party who liked to blame pretty much everything on Europe. And immigration. That nice Mr Farage, who led them, promised the British people the right to decide about Britain's future place in the European Union, if only they would vote for him in droves.

In what has to count as the biggest PR blunder in living memory, the then Prime Minister, David Cameron, with a general election looming and confidence in his party slipping away, promised that if he was re-elected, he would call a referendum on whether or not to remain in the EU. The decision would be left up to the British public.

Which is why it came to pass that there was a referendum, won by a narrow four per cent margin in favour of Brexit. The fact that at the time of voting there was a huge surge in Google searches for 'What is the EU?? and 'Where is the EU?' clearly had nothing to do with the outcome.

Now as I sit here stroking the cover of my lovely French passport and my French ID card, both giving my nationality as *Française*, I honestly am trying hard not to be smug. It's amazing how many people contacted me immediately after the vote to find out how they, too, could become French citizens. It's a pity so many of them hadn't hoisted in that you do actually have to be able to speak French to do so.

Of course Brexit hasn't actually happened, although some people seem to think it was instantaneous after the vote. At the moment, Britain is behaving a little like a cat. Wants out. You open the door. Wants in. And so on. Cue one of my dreaded earworms. I'm now humming The Clash's 1981 No. 1 hit single, 'Should I stay or should I go.'

It was exactly the same with the US presidential election. I kept telling everyone that Trump was going to win. Even when the polls were showing he had no chance. And yes, I do know polls are not always reliable. I've done market research to make a living before now, Mori trained, and I know the results are often skewed. But everyone was telling me I was wrong and it couldn't happen. I must have been the least surprised person I know when I woke up to the news that it had.

The spooky goings-on around my crime fiction books have become legendary. Without exception, every time I've brought out a new book, something I'd written about would happen in real life, either on the day of release or very shortly afterwards. I'm sure people thought it was just a massive publicity stunt on my part.

But how could I have known that on the day a book came out, an exact crime scene I'd mentioned in it would be taped off by the police as a real crime scene, where they'd found a body? That happened twice, with two different books and two separate places. And in case you're wondering, I never leave the Auvergne, so I didn't travel back to Stockport to plant the bodies. Nor can I afford a hit-man.

I have a fantastic team of betareaders for the crime books, whose job it is to spot any plot howlers. I'm pleased to have recently added a former police officer, someone I knew when I was younger, to the team, to help ensure procedural accuracy.

We were having a discussion via Messenger on Facebook and she mentioned something about my main character's police career which may have been easy to overlook and I had, admittedly, in the first six books, not touched on it quite enough. Imagine her surprise when I send her a passage I'd written just days before covering exactly that point.

I had yet another strange one, just as I was writing this chapter. The titles of my crime fiction books are all song titles, or lines from songs, and the title usually comes to me early on, in the form of an earworm. I'd started writing the seventh in the series at the same time as this book, and a song insinuated itself into my head and wouldn't go away.

It wouldn't do for a title; it was little known and the singer was not a big name, as I discovered when I mentioned to Doris, my Alpha betareader. She'd never heard of him. In one of those bizarre coincidences that haunt me, within the hour, there were two separate mentions of him on Twitter, one for winning some award or another, one as an A-list celebrity who had refused to appear at the Trump inauguration.

Despite all my witchy-woo powers, real or imagined, I didn't foresee what was heading my way next to wallop me over the head like a sandbag.

Things seemed to be progressing as they should with the house sale. My *notaire*, Mr France, had received the signed draft contract which enabled him to start moving ahead to wind up the French side of things. Now we'd separated out the French assets, his work was coming to an end. I'd included the two vehicles, the motorhome and the electric car, in with the house sale. He was gradually closing bank accounts so he was closer to a final figure on which to base my tax liability in France. Inheritance tax has to be paid within six months of the death here in France or hefty penalty charges are applied. Clearly it couldn't be paid until we had a final figure on which to base the sum I would owe. When he gave me his estimation of the tax liability, I was horrified. It was even more than I'd feared it would be, relying on my unreliable maths.

That didn't, unfortunately, mean that I would inherit a packet once the estate was wound up. Sadly, once the lawyers had taken their pickings and the outstanding bills had been paid, I'd be lucky to see my tax payment back, never mind anything else.

But I hate to be in debt, to anyone. It was in a rare moment of weak folly that I'd taken out a bank loan to have solar panels installed. And what a costly mistake that had turned out to be. They didn't generate anything like the amount I was told they would, leaving me with a huge shortfall between what they earned and what I was paying out on the bank loan.

I'd tried a court case – more expense – but we'd lost. In fact, there was a tiny victory in that the bank was ordered to pay me something towards my legal costs and to considerably reduce the interest I was paying on the loan. It still left me massively out of pocket.

Taxation is a thorny issue for most people. I don't believe anyone can put their hand on their heart and say with any conviction that they either enjoy or at least don't mind paying taxes. I'm basically in favour of everyone being taxed according to their means. But I do mean everyone. I don't like tax dodgers. They clearly care about no one other than themselves. A society needs a fair tax system so that everyone can benefit, in my humble opinion.

I particularly didn't want to be at odds with the French taxman, a ferocious beast who makes Smaug the Dragon from the Hobbit books seem about as scary as a fluffy, toothless old pussy-cat. I had some savings, though not a lot, and a few premium bonds. None of it brought me much of a return so I decided the sensible thing to do was to cash it all in and get the taxman off my back, for now, rather than wait for the final reckoning.

Because of the Brexit vote, the pound was volatile, to say the least, on the markets. I went through a currency transfer company, as they have far more idea than I do of how to get the best exchange rate. It wasn't brilliant, but it did mean I could send Me France a big chunk of what I owed in tax to show willing, and also to reduce interest charges.

I was feeling pleased with myself. I'd made some progress, in the right direction. I came back from yet another trip to the HHofH, my van loaded down with more stuff I'd decided to liberate. It was a good haul, too. A whole pallet full of expensive batteries to run solar systems more powerful than my camping ones for lighting. They'd been expensive, and there were eight of them. Heavy, of course, but I'd managed it.

When I get back to my house from any trip away, even a quick visit to the shops, I have my usual little *train-train*: dogs out, kettle on, laptop on, check emails and social media, check answerphone for any messages, which I tend to do online.

A bit worrying. A phone message from Mr Potential Buyer, saying there was a problem with the bank and he would try to call me again. I didn't like the sound of that. They had been so convinced that it would all go through quickly and that any delay would be on my side. I hoped it was not going to drag on too long. I was so looking forward to not having to do that drive any more.

I was just getting Leo the Lohberger going for the evening, to warm up the house and to cook my supper on, when the phone rang. The caller display showed me it was the Potential Buyers.

The news was worse than I feared. They had been turned down flat by the bank on their loan application. The sale was off. It was the husband on the phone. He told me his wife wanted to call me herself but she was crying so much at the disappointment that she couldn't speak.

Well, boo-hoo for her. I was not feeling exactly charitable, this late in the game. I'd just wasted four months with people who were clearly dreamers. The bank wouldn't advance them anything, not even a portion of what they'd asked for, so they were clearly not considered a good credit risk.

That meant I was now right back to square one. Ground

zero. With a big, empty house once again hanging round my neck like a millstone, and no immediate prospect of recouping what I'd already paid out to the taxman.

Chapter Twenty-six
And so to bed

With the sale dead in the water, I planned to do what I should have done from the start – put the house with an estate agent. I'd been nothing but accommodating to the Potential Buyers. Too much so, with hindsight. I'd made endless trips over there to let them in for estimates and surveys. I'd allowed them to bring all the children to view, so they could choose bedrooms. I could imagine they wouldn't be happy to hear, just before Christmas, that the deal was off.

Well, no more Ms Nice Tottie. I'd find a good agent, hand over the keys, and leave the rest up to them. Even if I finished up getting a bit less for the house, it would be worth it for the peace of mind. Not to mention reducing the number of times I had to make the journey over there.

I decided to go with the agency who had actually given the lower estimate. I'd been impressed with the boss lady, who had come herself to do the valuation. She knew the market well, they'd been in business for years, and she came highly recommended by a friend who lived nearby and knew of many people who had bought and sold through them. I made an appointment to go and see them to sort out all the paperwork and sign on the dotted line.

But first I'd had another enquiry about the king-sized bed I was selling, from the top floor guest room, and this one did sound reasonably serious. Quite a young man, by the sound of it, a pleasant voice. We nearly got off to a bad start when he left a message on my answerphone, after we'd already spoken a couple of times, saying he was interested in coming to see the bed but mentioning completely the wrong location to come to pick it up from.

I phoned him back, we sorted out where he was supposed to be going to, and I stressed once more that the mattress was far too big to fit in the back of even a large estate car. We fixed up a day and a time to meet at the HHofH. I wasn't overly optimistic, with the luck I'd had with selling things so far. But the trip wouldn't be wasted. There were still lots of things for me to bring back so I could get on with loading the back of the van while I waited for someone to arrive.

Not far off the appointed hour, a posh car pulled up at the gate and a young man got out to ask me if it was the right place for the bed. I could feel my hackles rising. It was a large car, but still a saloon car. There was no way a two-metre long orthopaedic mattress was going to fit in it, or balance on the roof.

I started to point this out but the young man, Fred, assured me that his parents were coming with a van to transport it, and they would be along shortly. Sure enough, before too long, a large white van pulled up outside. That was more like it.

The access to the HHofH is tricky. Goodness knows how my brother had managed to navigate the big motorhome, the Dingley, in and out so frequently without rolling it over down the hill. I told the driver that the safest way would be to drive in forwards then turn round on what had been the vegetable garden. The Potential Buyers had got the mini-digger driver to scrape it clear to make room to park the Dingley, so it could dig around in search of the missing *fosse septique*. There was room alongside, ideal for turning, and as there had been a sharp frost in the night, it was plenty hard enough so there was no risk of the van getting stuck.

All the women reading this book will immediately

understand what happens next. Is there any point in any woman trying to tell any man how to drive? I should have saved my breath. The next thing I saw was the driver attempting to back his van in through the narrow gates. It involves a short but steep slope, down, then up, and, as I could have predicted, as the van had a tow bar, as soon as the angle was right, the tow hitch grounded and got stuck so the van would go neither forward nor backwards. It was well and truly stuck.

The rear wheels were spinning, throwing up mud and grit everywhere, the engine was protesting, but budge it would not. Sticking out into the road at the front as it was, it was starting to present something of a traffic hazard. Not many vehicles go past but those that do tend to be whizzing along. What fun!

Each of them in turn had a go at driving the van. Father, mother, son. One would try driving while the other two shouted encouragement or criticism. All to no avail.

I'd seen it happen enough times before simply to go in search of some of the crazy paving slabs lying round to put under the back wheels, which had the desired effect.

I was hoping that, after such an inauspicious start, they were not going to waste my time haggling over the price of the bed, which was a steal. I just wanted rid of it. The emptier the house was, the easier it would be for future buyers to see its potential. The top storey master bedroom was large, but emptied of its large bed, it would look enormous.

In fact they appeared thrilled with their purchase, and there was no hint of a haggle. They also expressed an interest in the house itself, although I had the feeling it was just that, interest, rather than intent.

There was a fourth person with them and, as seems to happen quite often here, I never did find out who he was. He gave me the customary '*bonjour, madame*' and shook my hand, but no one told me if he was friend, family, or what. He'd been the one driving the car in which young Fred had arrived, so was clearly not just a passing stranger.

As we were walking past the glass doors to the sitting room to look at the bed, his eyes fell on my brother's piano. Mr Potential Buyer's brother had said he wanted to buy it, when he had come round to do the estimate for repairs and redecoration. No money was ever forthcoming from him, either, so I'd rather given up on him.

The eyes of the man with Fred the Bed lit up at the sight of it and he asked if he could have a look. It was horribly out of tune and needed a good clean-up, but he certainly knew his stuff as he was able to tinkle the ivories a bit. Unfortunately, he wasn't in the market for another piano, as he had one and no room for a second.

Because I could see he was genuinely interested, I took him down to the garage, in the dark and gloomy back corner of which lurked my brother's toy – the pianola. In its hey-day, it really had been a magnificent piece. It would give someone hours of amusement to restore and then have fun with, impressing their friends at dinner parties as my brother used to do, with the old 'Look, no hands' trick, whilst pedalling away with the feet.

Fred the Bed's friend was clearly interested. And tempted. But he kept coming back to the problem of having nowhere to store it and no expert knowledge of how to restore it. He promised to let me know, if ever he was interested, but I could tell it was a lost cause.

I was just going to have to bite the bullet and put it up on eBay for an attractive enough price for someone to take a punt on it. It was such a shame as it was a lovely piece of furniture, if nothing else. My problem was I had absolutely nowhere to store it, even if I could have transported it to my house. It was a hefty piece of kit, much heavier than a standard piano. My hayloft was by now absolutely full to bursting at the seams. Even if I could find room for it, I was worried that something that heavy would go straight through the rather fragile floor, as I had already done myself on one occasion. Then there was the woodworm problem in there. The pianola was such a beautiful old thing it would be criminal to let it get riddled with holes and start falling apart into dust. I needed to sell it directly, from where it was.

Now there was the disposal of another bed to sort out. The one I'd allowed the former Potential Buyers to store in the downstairs apartment as they had no room for it at their own house. They wanted it back, I think as a way to appease the daughter who was no longer getting the lovely bedroom with the huge walk-in wardrobe she had no doubt set her heart on. I wasn't being unreasonable. I was happy for them to collect it, but I would need to be there since, as soon as the purchase was off, I'd told them to put the keys in the letterbox so they no longer had access.

I arranged a time on a Sunday to go over to let them in to collect it. When I woke up on the day, it was a pea-souper of thick mist, not at all inviting for the drive over, plus I remembered, belatedly, that one of my books was featuring on a blog tour that day. I would need to spend pretty much the whole day on my computer sharing posts from Facebook and Twitter to get maximum possible exposure. I sent them an email to say I couldn't make it, but suggesting a day in the week when I would be available.

You'd think that, having just lost the house of their dreams through counting chickens before they hatched, the ex-buyers might have learnt a lesson. It seemed not. I got an email saying they'd already removed their daughter's old bed to make way for the new one and where was she supposed to sleep now? Then another one to say my suggestion of a weekday was no use as the husband and sons worked in the week so if I couldn't go at the weekend, they couldn't get their bed back.

Contrary to rumour, I'm actually quite a reasonable person, but that was just taking the pee somewhat. It's always a problem to get people to understand that those who are self-employed do actually work and have the same commitment to work times as salaried folk. Worse, when it comes to creative professions like writers, artists and the like, as we obviously just play all day. Not to mention the fact they I had kindly allowed them to store it there when I was not obliged to and I would have a three-hour drive there and back, depending on traffic, to go and let them in to get it.

Patiently, politely, I pointed out that I, too, had to work, often at the weekends. I said it would therefore be at a date and time which was convenient to me. I wasn't relishing the encounter. I would have preferred to have no more to do with them. But clearly the poor daughter couldn't carry on sleeping with their dogs, or wherever it was they had put her, having whisked her bed out from under her, if they were to be believed.

Chapter Twenty-seven
No timewasters, please

A phrase which often catches out tourists and newcomers to France is *hôtel de ville*. Many an unwary visitor has tried to book themselves into one for a night. But it's not the conveniently-placed boutique hotel they take it for, although it's often a rather grand-looking building. It's simply the name for a municipal building. The equivalent of a town hall or city hall, depending on the size of the conurbation where it's situated.

To add to the confusion, it's often referred to as the *mairie* instead. The estate agent where I had my appointment was situated in *Rue de l'Hôtel de Ville* in Châtel-Guyon, and the person I spoke to on the phone for directions told me it was on the right just after the *mairie*.

I've always been punctual, almost obsessively so. A lot of it stems from having lived in Germany for four years where almost everyone is on time. I've never known a more prompt nation. I don't know Châtel-Guyon well, so I allowed myself plenty of time to get there, find the right road, and somewhere to park, before my two-o'clock appointment.

Châtel-Guyon is a small town and *mairies* and *hôtels de ville* are usually well signposted, so what could possibly go wrong? Me being a muppet, is the usual answer to that question. I missed the sign so found myself taking a scenic but not very useful route up the little hills and narrow roads behind the casino and spa. Luckily I found a kind walker who, although not local himself, called down to a municipal worker tidying up the park at the bottom of the hill and between them they put me on the correct route.

Even after pausing for a cup of tea in my van – my little metal flask goes everywhere with me, and when it's not busy trying to scald me, it's a boon for hot drinks – I arrived early for my appointment. I was fully expecting to find the agency closed for the sacrosanct French lunchtime. Instead it was open and the woman who had done the valuation was there waiting for me, together with her husband.

They'd started the business together, nearly fifty years ago, so I assumed them to be in their early seventies at the least. Both were alert and sprightly and soon got started on preparing a dossier for the sale of the Hammer House of Horrors. The back office we used for some of the paperwork was fascinating. There was a glass panel inset into the floor revealing a beautifully restored old well, which water of incredible clarity.

Madame told me they would only take on the Hammer House of Horrors if they had it exclusively and Domi had put me under strict instructions not to sign an exclusive deal. Looking around the office, seeing how they handled things, and having checked them out online and in various publications, I decided to ignore the advice and sign them up for six months exclusivity.

What I liked best of all was what they did to avoid wasted viewings. It's impossible to legislate for all timewasters but at least they did everything within their power. Madame told me that they prepared a detailed dossier for potential viewers, including up to sixty photographs, so they were in no doubt as to what they were going to see.

The question of their fees was also better news than I had anticipated. I'd always understood that both buyer and seller paid a portion of the fees. Madame asked me what figure I wanted to get. I said the same as had been on offer from the failed sale. She took the figure, added on her commission from a predetermined scale and that would be the asking price. She was confident they would get it, too.

I'd arranged to have duplicate keys cut to all the doors but asked if someone could meet me at the house two days later so I could show them how the locks worked. One of my brother's schemes had been to start building a sort of porch-cum-conservatory under the overhanging roof of the front door, extending the length of the living room. He'd bought a job lot of double glazed doors but, as ever, with any of his plans, there were drawbacks. One of the doors he'd used, the one which was the entry point, had a peculiar locking system. For a start, there was no handle on the inside, so it was easy to get yourself shut in. The doors, and therefore their keys, were Italian. When Domi had kindly tried to get a duplicate cut for me, the key-cutter she went to said he couldn't do it as he didn't have a master which corresponded.

I wanted to keep a set of keys for myself, so I could continue to go back to carry on clearing it out. But I didn't want to risk the estate agent managing to lock himself and any viewers in between the outer door and main inner door with no way of getting out. It would be embarrassing and probably not conducive to a sale.

I could see from the looks he was giving me that he thought I was being patronising, suggesting he might not be able to figure out locking mechanisms himself. I was vindicated when he visited, though. Having carefully told him that pushing the button at the same time as turning the handle would lock the door, so to make sure he had the keys in his hand before doing so, he managed to lock himself out a couple of times before he got the hang of it.

My sense of humour gets me into a lot of trouble. No matter how many smileys, winkies or exclamation marks I put on social media posts, not to mention 'hashtag just kidding' or similar, someone, somewhere, will always take me seriously and go off on a rant about what I've posted.

The humour tends to be of the decidedly mischievous sort, with a bit of prodding of wasps' nests. Interestingly, the French word for mischievous is '*malicieux*'. There's never any intended malice in my little games, but I do love to play them.

Take, for example, my famous answerphone message when I had my remote riding centre on top of an isolated Welsh plateau, where I lived alone, most of the time. I thought most people ringing me up would realise that: 'I'm sorry I can't come to the phone right now. I'm exercising the Rottweilers while my boyfriend, who's home on leave from the SAS, is in the gun room cleaning the Purdeys', was a joke. A tongue-in-cheek warning to potential burglars who might be phoning up to see if anyone was at home. But one anxious parent, trying to book a residential riding holiday for her daughter, phoned back, most anxious to know if her child would be safe with big dogs and firearms about.

I'd told the agents about my potential sale which had fallen through. They wanted to know the name of the buyers, which I told them. The son knew the name and, after checking on the computer system, found that they had shown them other properties, earlier in the year, but at a significantly lower price than the one at which I was selling. In other words, had I gone to the agents in the first place, they would have known that the Potential Buyers were punching above their weight and bidding above their budget.

I wasn't looking forward to the forthcoming meeting with the ex-buyers when they came to collect the bed. So the mischievous part of me couldn't resist arranging the appointment with the agent at the exact time that the bed collection was scheduled to happen. When they saw him there, they would know that I knew the real story about them and their purchasing power.

The agent was as punctual as I had been to my interview at his office, which was a good start. After we'd done the fiddling about with the locks and I was happy that he'd mastered the art, he asked for a look around. There was no sign of the bed collectors, so we got on with it.

He certainly knew his stuff, that much was sure. Even though I'd by now emptied out a ton of junk, with the help of the two Jills, not to mention shovelling up all the cat mess, it was still far from pristine. But he saw straight past the worst of it, commenting instead that it was a solid, well-built house with no signs of damp, and that all the work needing doing was largely cosmetic. This was great. He said it with conviction. I believed him. I nearly made him an offer on the place, he was so convincing.

At that moment, as we were in the garage and the cellar rooms beyond, we heard voices and I saw Mr Ex-Buyer in the open garage doorway. Who should be with him but *Monsieur Le Maire*. Clearly the bed was a two-person lift, but I was surprised he'd chosen the mayor to come with him and not his brother, or one of his sons. I wondered if he'd not been looking forward to facing me and had needed moral support. The cynical part of me wondered if it had been going to be a last-ditch attempt to get me to drop the price so the purchase could still go ahead. No chance!

I was genuinely busy with the agent so I didn't have chance to say more than a *bonjour* and an *au revoir* to the failed buyer. He seemed quite relieved to be able to slope off as soon as possible. *Monsieur Le Maire* made a point of coming to shake my hand, to wish me a merry Christmas and a happy New Year. He kept hold of my hand while doing so and looked me directly in the eyes in what was clearly his local politician sincere look. I may be doing him an injustice but it rang false to me. I couldn't detect any warmth in his eyes.

I'd been in the process of trying to load a big, solid copper water tank into my van when they'd all arrived. It was a bit of a monster. One of my brother's brilliant ideas. He planned to use it to have hot water from a series of solar panels, but it also had fittings for a gas supply and for an electric immersion heater.

Theoretically, it would mean he would always have hot water by some means or another. Of course, he'd never got as far as fitting it anywhere. The date on it was 2004 so he'd clearly bought it for his old place in Wales, as that was two years before we'd even started looking at French property.

It was far too big for my house and therefore not an economical prospect to fit. But the scrap value of copper was such that it would be worth a bob or two. The trouble was, it was taller than I am and too wide for me to get my arms round it to get a decent purchase.

Mr Estate Agent said he had time to spare before his next appointment so insisted on helping me to load it, and anything else heavy which needed shifting. I was certainly not going to refuse. I'd already loaded the rest of the big batteries, which had about finished me off, so I was delighted to let him move two big cases of old LP records. I'd no idea how heavy they could be. I doubted I'd find any true old classics, worth a fortune, but I didn't want to throw them away without checking.

When we'd finished that and he was ready to leave, he too shook my hand to say his farewells and to assure me that he would do all in his power to find me a genuine buyer. He too held eye contact while he was saying it.

Somehow, his look was much more warm and sincere. I came away feeling more positive than I had since the sale fell through. Perhaps my luck was about to change for the better.

Chapter Twenty-eight
Risk assessment – High

I couldn't write any book with me in it without mentioning the catastrophes which befall me on a regular basis in daily life. For one thing, no one who knows me would believe that I had gone more than a year, since I wrote the last Sell the Pig book, without some accident or another.

The ironic thing is that in a previous life, I was qualified in Risk Assessment and Management, responsible for Health and Safety at work, and doing all the pre-planning to ensure the safety of competitors and spectators at large horse shows. These days, I'm doing well if I make a cup of tea without inflicting some kind of injury on myself.

Remember my second-degree burn from my trusty flask? The one I threw out to ensure that I didn't do the same thing again? I bought myself a new one, so it couldn't happen. The clever sort, where you don't have to remove the stopper to pour, you just have to depress a button on the top. What sort of a silly tart would forget to press the button again so that it wasn't in pouring mode before carrying it? And surely no one would be careless enough to inflict exactly the same burn, on the same hand, in the same place?

Oops! Guilty as charged. At least this time, I knew how to deal with the big liquid blister which resulted, and still had plenty of the right sort of dressings from the last episode.

The Curious Incident of the Loft Ladder in the Night-time

was in a class of its own. When I'd first had the grottage done up and made habitable, before I moved in full-time, I'd got the builders to put a floor in the loft to the main house, as it would make a useful storage area. There wasn't the head-room to do much more with it. I instructed Patrick, the handyman, to put a good layer of insulation between the floor and the tongue and groove ceilings he was installing in the bedrooms and bathrooms, then we discussed where to put the access and what to use.

The builders had left an opening on the tiny landing just above the steep staircase. With my responsible risk assessor's hat on, I wasn't keen on that. Falling out of the loft would be one thing; The ceilings are quite low so it wouldn't be much of a fall. But that location would then give me the possibility of tumbling on down the stairs as well, which was probably better avoided.

Instead we settled for putting in a folding ladder on the narrow passage to the guest bedroom. There was just about enough room, although it meant opening the door to the room every time I went up there. The ladder had a pull down flap, on strong steel springs, then the steep wooden ladder unfolded from inside it. The space which was available for us to install one at all was limited so it was a case of getting whichever one would fit.

For some reason, I never had a lot of confidence in that ladder. Whenever I climbed up it, I always imagined it would suddenly fold itself up with me inside it, guillotining off the fingers with which I clung to it as I made my perilous ascent. Perilous because the steps are steep and shallow and I have big feet. My mother always unkindly referred to them as canal barges.

I was right to anticipate an assassination attempt by the loft ladder. I was wrong in how I had imagined it would happen. One day as I was pulling it down for the ascent, there was a loud crack, a flying piece of metal hit me in the face and the whole heavy contraption fell down on one side, narrowly missing my head. In fact, the flying piece of metal was a blessing in disguise as it had caused me instinctively to stagger backwards and had probably spared me a serious head injury.

The flying metal hadn't inflicted any real damage, just a sore upper lip. I was thankful it hadn't connected with my expensive glasses, which were not insured for such damage. I could see that it was, in fact, the metal arm to which one of the springs had been attached, and it had snapped off. Metal fatigue, presumably. But now I had a problem. With it no longer being spring-loaded, it was heavy to push back up, and wouldn't stay in place on its own. I would need to prop it with a length of wood because leaving it open was going to be cold, especially now the winter frosts had started.

I found a wooden prop to do a temporary job. It was slightly too long so had to go at an angle, which left it jutting out slightly on the landing. Risk assessment, remember? I could see myself tripping over that jutting end on night-time trips to the bathroom, so I tied a bright red sock round it to remind me. Then as a double measure, I put the other red sock on the end of the handrail on the stairs, at the top.

Well, I pulled that one partway on then left it dangling so that it looked like an unsuccessful attempt to put on a... Now if you're giggling at this point, you have a mucky mind, because I was going to say trying to pull a sock on to someone else's foot!

Of course, I overlooked the obvious flaw in my cunning plan. I often stagger to the loo on autopilot in the night without bothering to put the light on, so I can't see a thing, not sticking out wooden props, certainly not red socks. Cue painful stubbed toes and the trap door falling down with such a noise I'm surprised it didn't bring my neighbour rushing round to see what was happening. Mercifully, it missed falling on me, but it did prompt me to do a proper job, with two props, cut to the correct length so they were vertical and close to the side walls.

One of my more amusing incidents came when I decided once and for all that it was time to evict the Ginger Interloper from the barn. That cat had decided he was there to stay and didn't even bother to venture outside any more. He would just sit there, waiting for food. Then he'd go and crap anywhere and everywhere, ignoring the many available litter trays. House-trained he clearly was not and I'd had about enough of cat poo for one year, thank you very much.

I'd taken to calling him Schrödinger, but that did not mean, as some on social media assumed, that I was in any way adopting him. It was simply that he was something of a paradox. Like the cat in the thought experiment, which was both dead and alive inside the box, the Ginger Intruder was both inside and outside the barn.

I finally succeeded in catching him one day, carefully lifting him by the scruff and depositing him gently but firmly outside Al-Cat-Traz to make it clear to him that he had outstayed his welcome. I then shut the trap door but left the door to the hayloft open so that HRH and Bibi could still enjoy the sunshine of the upper deck without our unwelcome guest being able to get back in. My latest efforts had finally thwarted even the determined Bibi, so I was sure my theory would hold good. Eternal optimist, remember?

Only when I went back in to feed them later that day, who should be sitting there smiling at me once more? Correct! But how the heck did he get back in?

The barn is large – a bigger footprint than the grottage itself – and solidly built. It's attached to the house at one side with no way in at all, only the cellar door, which is always firmly shut unless I am going in or out of it. The first part is a large tractor shed, with massive double wooden doors at either end. They are sound and secure, with no holes or gaps anywhere.

Next to it, on the lower level, is the old cowshed, now cleared out and used as the dog's squash court, for ball games when it's wet outside. There was a gap at the top of the wall to that, under the hayloft floor, but I'd carefully blocked that with stout planks of wood which were all still nailed in place. I checked carefully.

The hayloft itself had a door into Al-Cat-Traz but other than that, there was no way in or out, or Bibi would have found it. Yet here was the Ginger Intruder, once again. And the situation was to repeat itself a few more times before he got too wily to allow me near enough to grab him any more. I was starting to wonder if there were identical twin cats, one inside and one outside the barn. Either that or I was completely losing what remained of my marbles.

Then I spotted it. There was a small gap in one part of the roof of Al-Cat-Traz where I'd run out of wire mesh and hadn't bothered as it was up against the wall and there was no purchase there for even a cat as determined as Bibi to climb up and out of it. Of course, I hadn't constructed it with keeping intruders out in mind, just on keeping the girls in.

It was easily fixed with a couple of sections of wood, a hammer and a few nails. Bish-bash-bosh. Job's a good 'un. Now all I had to do was to get the interloper back out again. Some hopes. I couldn't even manage to manoeuvre so that he was between me and the door so I could shoo him out. He was far too wary now, and clearly knew what my intention was. It would require cunning.

I store my firewood in the tractor shed, right down one length of it. Ten steres (cubic metres) to be precise, although that is going down as winter advances. It's up against the side of the cow shed and the hayloft. But the only way I could manage to sneak round and get behind That Darn Cat was first to clamber over the log pile, then to wriggle my way through cement mixer, pair of wooden gates, several chainsaws, eight dining tables, enough crockery to open a restaurant, a cuddly toy – you get the picture.

Apart from the risk to life and limb, impossible to accomplish quietly, especially as I kept falling over things.

Which simply made the Ginger-job scuttle into hiding in a dark corner. I did eventually manage to reach the hayloft door, having totally forgotten that Al-Cat-Traz was too secure to allow even a cat to get out of, never mind me. So I had to do the even more perilous return journey, trying not to bring the log pile down on top of me.

Eventually, by putting food out on the deck and lying in wait with a long rope tied to the door handle, I managed to tempt him outside and slam the door shut behind him. Peace is restored. Back to two cats again, and Bibi and HRH are clearly thrilled to have their barn back to themselves once more, and no-one to share their food.

The Ginger-job is still around, as I am not heartless enough to have thrown him out with no means of support, certainly not in winter. There is food, water and a warm bed for him in the cellar, and the same in the next-door neighbour's accessible woodstore. He is thriving, being well fed in both places. I have yet to think of a way to let my two come and go at will without letting him back in to the barn.

Chapter Twenty-nine
That was the year that was

2016 is going to go down in many people's memories as the year the Grim Reaper was on a productivity bonus. Celebrities were dropping like flies. From musical legends like David Bowie, Prince and Leonard Cohen, to actors such as Alan Rickman and Frank Finlay, sporting legends like Muhammed Ali and TV stars including Terry Wogan and Victoria Wood.

There were probably no more deaths than in an average year. It's just that the names were big hitters, and they seemed to come thick and fast. The public were going crazy, wallowing in grief for people they never knew as if they were close friends. Yes, it was sad that Debbie Reynolds died the day after her daughter, but she was 84. Some of us were dealing with the loss of family members who were much younger.

I did, however, feel something of a link to Sir Terry Wogan. I, along with thousands of others of middle years and upwards, spent many a morning hour listening to him on Wake Up to Wogan, and were enthusiastic TOGs – Terry's Old Geezers/Gals. We would write or fax in our thoughts (long before emails) in the hopes he would read out our ramblings, which would earn us the honour of a TOGs sweatshirt, emblazoned with the group slogan, 'Do I come here often?'

In a recent attempt to clear out the chaos in my loft, before the treacherous ladder prevented further access, I found the letter to Sir Tel which had won me the coveted prize. It was a standing joke on the show, which all who wrote in shared, that there was only one other listener apart from them, although it was a hugely popular morning show.

'I finally have the proof positive you seem to require of my official TOG status and my proof far outweighs all that of your other listener, so I definitely qualify for a sweaty shirt (medium size).

I have just had a letter from good old Tom Champagne, prize draw manager of Reader's Digest (dear old Tom, he writes to me so often, we're almost like pen-pals) thanking me for my loyal custom since I placed my first order with them on January 1st 1900.

'On my reckoning, if I was ordering books 97 years ago, I must be well past my century and as I never got the royal telegram, I will just have to settle for one of your fashion statements.'

My personal favourite, however, was one I heard him reading out as I was driving in to work one morning, when I lived in the New Forest. Or rather, trying to read it out. Dear Sir Tel was always a terrible giggler, prone to corpsing over anything funny and being unable to continue. He had various regular newsreaders who joined him on his slot and he always had nicknames for them such as Alan Dedicoat, who was always known as Deadly Alancoat or simply Deadly.

I do remember it took him rather a long time to get through my fax, in between snorting, whimpering and crying with laughter.

'Dear Terry Wogan, Would you mind not whistling like a demented budgie whilst playing records? I travel to work between 7.40 and 7.50 each day and am forced to listen to your rubbish as my car radio is permanently stuck on Radio Two.

'This morning whilst playing 'Dream a Little Dream', you and Deadly started chirruping away, totally driving my border collie, Meic, to distraction. Do you not realise that every whistle gives a signal to a highly trained sheepdog? In the space of that one track, you whistled Come Bye, Away to Me, Lie Down, Stand, Walk On, Get Back and That'll Do.

'The contortions poor Meic went through to accomplish all that in the confines of a Renault 21, with another dog in it, were pitiful to see, so please cease forthwith.'

Another milestone for me was that 2016 was the year I took up planking. Why? Because it seemed like a good idea at the time. It's one of those torture exercises designed to improve core strength and I decided that mine could definitely do with a bit of help.

I'd started the year determined to make an effort to keep fit. Or at least as fit as someone approaching their mid sixties with a couple of spinal injuries could be. I'd started out trying to maintain my ten thousand steps a day, for which I'd bought myself a simple belt-mounted step counter. Three, to be precise, as I kept losing them.

Writing as much as I do, not to mention gossiping for hours on Facebook, I do spend rather too much time sitting in front of my computer. Long walks with the dogs had been a bit curtailed because of the problems with Scribble and also Fleur getting increasingly more vocal on car journeys. They still got plenty of exercise, but a lot of it consisted of me standing still and throwing balls for them in the garden or their squash court. Actually, as Rosie has never mastered the art of bring the ball all the way back to me, she still saw to it that I did do quite a bit of walking about, though nothing like ten thousand steps.

Someone I follow on Facebook posted something about this '30-day planking challenge.' It looked a doddle to me, I couldn't see what all the fuss was about. You lay on the floor, arms bent, then simply pushed yourself up, as if starting a press-up, but on forearms and tiptoes, then held the position for as long as the training pattern dictated.

How hard could that be? I thought, with my customary arrogance and optimism.

In the 30-day plan, you started off with ten seconds then built up progressively to a minute. Despite my age and decrepitude, I still consider myself fairly fit. I've lived on my own for a long time and am used to wrestling with all sorts of things single-handedly, including the daily hauling of firewood logs for Leo the Lohberger. I would waltz it, I thought.

When, five seconds after starting my first attempt, I collapsed in a heap of trembly muscles on the floor, I realised it was not quite as easy as I thought. I did persist, and got to the point of being able to do sixty seconds at a time every day.

It all went a bit by the wayside when the house sale collapsed. I'd rather lost the morale to do anything much and I have a morbid fear of failure. If I tried to do it and didn't succeed, that would mean seven years bad luck. Or a plague of locusts. Or something. I will get back into it, but I suspect I might have to start again from the ten-second mark and build back up.

Quite by chance, I hit on a brilliant keep-fit scheme which was also a valuable dog training aid. I advertised The Dingley (the old motorhome) for sale on *Le Bon Coin.* To say I was swamped with calls was an understatement. It was a non-stop onslaught. The minute I put the phone down there was another call and it went on like that for ages, until in the end I simply had to unplug the phone to get some peace.

Best of all, people were emailing me and were actually bidding above what I was advertising it for, and it's not an auction site, so I arranged a viewing for one cash buyer. I'd pitched the price low of necessity. Without a test certificate, I couldn't re-register it nor was I legally allowed to sell it as a 'goer'. It would have to be sold at scrap value, 'for spare parts'.

I also discovered, when I was rooting through documents trying to find its log book, that it was actually a condemned vehicle. My brother had mentioned he'd been stopped by the police because the side door had broken hinges and had decided to fly open just as a police vehicle was driving behind him. He'd made light of it so I didn't realise it meant that it would have to be certified by someone from a panel of experts as roadworthy before it could once more be driven legally on the public highway.

By one of those bizarre coincidences, I also had a phone call from someone interested in the tuk-tuk, the little electric car, and wanting to come at the same time as the person for the motorhome. I'd had great difficulty in explaining to people that I couldn't tell them if the tuk-tuk was a goer or not. Being an electric car, it needed to be plugged into the mains to be charged up. The electricity was off at the HHofH and it was impossible to get it anywhere else to charge it.

So how do phone calls amount to dog training? For reasons best known to her, Fleur has always barked when the phone goes. With the calls coming so thick and fast, she simply decided it was all too much trouble so started completely ignoring the strident bell.

Again, I explained as patiently as I could to the person interested in the tuk-tuk that I was selling it for rock-bottom scrap value as I was making no claim for it being in running order. Second-hand cars tend to be pricey in France, often higher than UK prices, so people should have realised that it's not possible to pick up a runner for a mere three hundred quid or so.

Nothing was going to be easy with those vehicles. Not only was the motorhome in a bad way, so was its paperwork, I discovered. Unfortunately just after two men had driven up from the south to buy it unseen. It all got a bit ugly for a moment, but it was as much their fault as mine, once again expecting something advertised dirt cheap for spare parts was going to be roadworthy.

But it did at least look as if things were starting to sell once more, after the festivities. And there was better to come. I'd only given the instructions and the keys to the estate agent a day before they closed for a week's break over Christmas and the New Year so I hadn't expected miracles. I'd had a couple of people phone me wanting to view privately. That would save them money, by cutting out the agents' fees, but had no benefit to me. Quite the reverse. It meant more trips over there to show them round and the prospect of dealing with more timewasters. I simply referred them to the agent.

New Year's Day was a Sunday in 2016, but unlike in the UK, the Monday doesn't then become a Bank Holiday in France. It's business as usual. And it was late Monday morning that the agent phoned to say he had shown his first potential buyer round and they were going to let him know by the end of the day whether or not they were interested.

They did. They were. They came back with a slightly cheeky offer. I told the agent to try to push it up a bit, although he was not confident. Then I had to sweat it out for nearly twenty-four hours. The following day I was meeting up with my friend Muta in one of our favourite cafés. She'd been away for nearly six weeks, on a trip back to England, so we had a lot of catching up to do.

My mobile phone was in the pocket of my fleece, flung on to the seat next to me. So when it began to ring, I nearly jumped out of my skin and started scrabbling round frantically to find it. Muta, who had no idea of the significance of the call, thought I was having some sort of attack.

The news was all good. The buyer had capitulated and would pay the price I wanted. They had checked out his finances and they were sound. And he'd already signed the '*proposition d'achat*', proposal to buy.

Could it be that 2017 was going to be a better year, at last?

Chapter Thirty
Is that Billinge Lump?

I can't believe it's been nearly a year already since my brother died. Just days short of nine months, to be precise. I've still not got past the stage of half-expecting an email from him to pop up in my inbox. Especially on the first of every month.

Losing a family member is never easy, for anyone. What's made this harder is knowing how upset he would have been had he realised how much stress – and work – he would cause me in leaving everything to me.

But my brother – Pete, to his few friends – was now beyond the worries of this mortal life. He was no longer being hounded for unpaid bills, illegally-running vehicles or any of the other mundane cares he'd been struggling with. Instead I'm trying to write this whilst being bombarded by idiot emails, as I've removed my phone number from the advert now, trying to buy the Dingley for a song without realising that it's cheap because it's not roadworthy so no, they can't drive it back to Clermont-Ferrand or the south of France or even the end of the road.

Pete was beyond all of this hassle because he had now gone 'home'. Back to St Helens, where he was born. Back, in fact, to that most iconic place of our childhood, Billinge Lump. Scene of many a blackberry forage as a family, listening to our granny grumbling about the 'thieving pickers' who had dared to be there before us to 'steal' the best of the crop.

I'd entrusted him, for his final journey, to his best friend, Neil, and to another old friend, Jock, who were going to take him on a proper lads' road trip and make an occasion of it. So it's over to the two of them now, to continue with the tale.

'We left Wales at half past eight on an overcast but humid day at the end of August. Pete was sitting happily in the back of the camper, where he'd spent the night, prior to his last road trip.

'We were going on a route Pete had taken many times, driving up to Stockport to see his mother, passing some of the places where he used to like to stop. We stopped for a brew and some snacks at one of them, the Sugar Loaf Mountain, near Brecon.

'The sun came out as we continued on our way, crossing the border from England to Wales just before two in the afternoon. We got to the village of Billinge just before four. We asked for directions from the local bakers' about how to get up to the highest point. It seemed to be a popular place, with a lot of people coming and going, and one couple looking as if they were bedding down for the night. We thought we might get a few strange looks, scattering ashes up there, so looked for a quiet spot.

'We took Pete for a last photoshoot in the field in front of the tower at the summit while we waited for the couple to move on. His sister had told us there were many old family photos posed in front of that building.

'We sat enjoying the sun and toasting Pete with a gin and tonic, his favourite drink. As we sat there, two plane vapour trails crossed above us. X marks the spot. It must have been Pete agreeing to his final resting place. So we scattered his ashes just near the tower, between a gorse bush and a broom and poured a gin and tonic, his last drink, over his final resting place.'

Jock – 'Neil played Con Te Partirò, Andrea Bocelli, because it had been played at Pete's funeral and was a favourite of his. Some passers-by commented that they thought we were going to dance.'

Neil – 'We said our farewells to Pete and left him to enjoy the beautiful sunset while we went off to have a meal out, paid for by him. He'd always loved going for meals out; it had been part of every trip we went on together, so it was a fitting final tribute.'

Jock – 'As Pete was ex-Royal Fleet Auxiliary, we decided it would be fitting to rinse out the residual ashes from the urn in the sea, when we got back to Wales, at Burry Port, where he often went. We found a quiet and secluded part of the beach overlooking the North Gower peninsula, a designated area of outstanding natural beauty. It's a tranquil place, where we can go and remember Pete whenever we want to, and it's near to where he lived in Wales.'

Neil – 'The last thing to do now is to plant up the urn with something which will flower in remembrance of Pete.'

As I sit here, reading through the notes of these two friends, I can almost imagine being there with them. Neil's a professional photographer so he took lots of photos of every stage of their trip, including the cover shot for this book. It's nice to think that in some way, my brother might have known about it and enjoyed it all.

My brother had some good times in his life, but a lot of it wasn't happy. I hope he's happy now, wherever he is. Sometimes I remember fun times we had together, and there were a fair few of those. Then memories sneak up on me and leak out of my eyes.

But hopefully, he's at peace now and some time soon, everything will be sorted and I can start to get back to my own little *train-train*. Once the bills stop thudding into my letterbox.

This time it is the end of the Sell the Pig series. Really the end. The next memoirs will have to be from further back. Did I ever tell you about being snowed up alone on a Welsh mountain with no water, electricity or telephone for three weeks? Perhaps I will. One day.

But for now, as my mother would have said, with her usual dramatic delivery:

THE END